Trade **HOA** Stress for **Success**

A Guide to Managing Your HOA in a Healthy Manner

Richard Thompson and Doug McLain
with Erik Wecks

First Published in the United States of America
Copyright © 2014 Richard Thompson, Doug McLain, Erik Wecks
All Rights Reserved.

ISBN: 978-0692354162

Table of Contents

One:
Getting the Focus Right

Serving on your homeowner association (HOA) board can be a thankless and lonely job. It often feels like a no-one-wanted-it-and-I-got-stuck-with-it kind of position. More often than it ought, the job description comes with midnight maintenance phone calls, long-winded alcohol-induced suggestions, and the expectation that it's your job to deal with the noisy neighbors next door. You end up feeling much more like the person designated to put out fires than a board member. Perhaps a better description might be a janitor. When you serve on a board, it feels like you're always picking up other people's garbage (and dog poop).

It ought not to be this way. These activities should never be thought of as the proper responsibility of a board member. Neither is enforcing rules, making collection phone calls, or writing citations. HOAs are too small for neighbors to be treating neighbors in this fashion.

Volunteering for your HOA board should be a rewarding experience. This book won't help you find the best strategies to make sure all the garbage cans are off the curb by 6:01 PM on Thursday. If you busy yourself with such matters on your board, we encourage you to reconsider. It isn't any fun to live under an HOA board that concerns itself with finding every reason it can to fine its members. Such attitudes undermine the whole point of the HOA, turning "care-free living" into a nightmare for the owners. If, on the other hand, you want to learn how to protect your HOA, create a sense of community, and look back with pride on your time on the board, this book is for you.

Getting the Focus Right

Too often, boards spend large amounts of time focused on relatively unimportant matters, while weightier matters get ignored.

They get caught arguing about an endless stream of minor issues and lose the thread of their responsibilities. They skimp on items like reserves or insurance to keep their fees as low as possible, and then use special assessments to do their maintenance. Or they neglect basic safety measures and allow one person to handle all the cash for the organization with little to no oversight. In our work, we run across a disturbing number of boards that find themselves in very deep water because their choices led to trouble down the road. Somewhere they got lost in minutiae, and important things—like filing tax returns—didn't get done.

Your board exists to administer the business of an HOA charged to care for millions of dollars in assets—the homes of its members. The homes in your HOA not only represent the dreams and desires of your residents, they are often the single greatest investment the owners will ever make. Maintaining the value of these investments through the proper management of the HOA is the serious business of the board. It's the reason the board exists.

As a board member, you have a similar role to that of a board member of a Fortune 500 company. Homeowners are the shareholders in the company—they have a stake in the outcome of your decisions and your oversight, but they do not run the company. The board of a Fortune 500 company may hold the ultimate financial (or fiduciary) responsibility for the health of a company. However, just like an HOA board, it does not handle the day-to-day work of the company. Rather, it sets direction and policy. It oversees and hires those who will do the work of the company. We find that task-oriented boards that conduct themselves in a fashion similar to corporate boards outshine boards that make it their job to micro-manage every aspect of HOA business. They also make serving on the board a much more rewarding experience.

However, there is one major difference between the board of a Fortune 500 company and an HOA board. A corporate board is often filled with executives and experienced business people who have worked at all levels within a corporation. They understand the ins and outs of what it takes to manage a company. In contrast, most board members are not experts in HOA finance, management, or taxes.

You don't need to become an expert to serve on the board— mostly it's just common sense. However, a good board does know the signs of trouble to look for and pitfalls to avoid to make sure its members' experience is as rewarding as possible. We don't intend to make you an expert, but we will make sure you know when you need an expert.

We want you to see this book as a compass needle pointing toward a better way to think and act as a board. The end result will be a board experience that is radically different than the one experienced by many board members. Instead of running from crisis to crisis, we want your time of service to be marked by specific, measurable accomplishments and improvements to the health of your HOA.

Along the way, we want to help point out major pitfalls that damage many HOAs. Avoiding these potential disasters will mean being a little more cautious and methodical than many boards. Think of it this way—you may ride in a car for years without getting in an accident, but the consequences when one comes make it worthwhile to put on your seatbelt every time you get in. So, in that sense, you can also consider this book your seatbelt.

Where We Are Heading

In order to make your experience on the board rewarding, we need to start our book by taking a deeper look into your role as a board member, the way in which a board should properly function, and the relationship between the board and its membership. Once a board understands its role, it still has to deal with getting the work done on a monthly basis. We are strong believers that neighbors shouldn't collect fees from or enforce rules on their neighbors. Every board—no matter how small—should have a relationship of some sort with a professional manager. We'll look at the reasons for this and give you the tools you will need to pick a great management company. Then, we'll look closely at some specific issues that often hang up boards and wreck the experience of serving—things like handling special assessments, meetings, rentals, and rule enforcement. Managing the finances of the HOA takes up a large portion of a board's time. Toward the end of the book, we'll look at the financial issues a board faces, including items like reserve studies, budgeting, and the cash controls necessary to help prevent embezzlement. Finally, we'll make sure you have a basic primer on taxes, so that you can avoid the costly mistakes that regularly lead the IRS to send out tax bills to HOAs for hundreds of thousands of dollars.

Two:
A Better Vision for Your
Board

We've already stated in the introduction that we believe an HOA board should see itself like a board of a large corporation. It should set policy and provide oversight. As much as possible, it should avoid being involved in the day-to-day affairs of the HOA. We recognize that for many boards, this will mean a significant change in the way in which they function.

In this chapter, we want to take a step backward and lay the groundwork for our assertion. We also want to give you a few key concrete steps you can take to start changing the way your board behaves. Finally, we want to make our case for how looking at your HOA board in a similar fashion to a corporate board can help create a better HOA. To start, though, we need to make sure everyone understands the nature of the beast. Just what is an HOA anyway?

What Is a Homeowner Association?

So just what do we, the authors, mean when we say the words "homeowner association"? We use the term HOA in the broadest possible manner. We mean any mandatory membership organization in which membership is based upon common ownership of real estate. There are all sorts of HOAs, including condominium associations, town-home developments, and planned communities of single-family homes. In our book, all of these are covered under the single term HOA. The tie that holds them all together is that the deed for the property requires the owner to be part of the association and abide by its rules.

There are two major benefits offered to homeowners in exchange for their willingness to be part of the HOA. First, the HOA exists to share amenities for homeowners that they couldn't afford on their own—for instance, fitness and swimming facilities or a common room. These amenities add value to the real estate included in the HOA.

The second and more central purpose of these HOAs is to preserve and protect the value of the members' real estate. It accomplishes this task by maintaining the common property and enforcing reasonable rules intended to keep residents from doing anything that might be detrimental to their neighbors.

The specific responsibilities of an HOA can vary widely. On the one end, you might have an HOA tasked with simply maintaining the sign at the front of the development and a few basic rules. On the other end, you can have huge HOAs with tens of thousands of residents and hundreds of employees. Like a fingerprint, each HOA is unique in the makeup of its residents and its responsibilities.

The rules and responsibilities are laid out in the governing documents of the HOA. In many cases, the governing documents begin with state laws that regulate the ways in which HOAs handle their responsibilities. This is particularly true for condominiums. All fifty states have some sort of condominium act on the books. Most of these acts lay out the basics of how to run a condominium association, including the frequency of owner meetings, the minimum qualifications for a board, and the basic rights and responsibilities of owners. On the other hand, many planned developments of single-family homes are governed almost solely by the restrictions placed in the deed by the developer at the time of construction, commonly known as CC&Rs (Covenants, Conditions and Restrictions). However, this is changing in some states, as governments argue they have an interest in preserving the property values of homes within their states. Some states are passing legislation similar to the condominium acts for single-family HOAs.

Governing Documents

If a board would like to run its HOA in a professional manner, then it must become intimately familiar with its governing documents. These are the documents that outline the board's responsibilities and the scope of its authority. However, most of the time these documents have been drafted by attorneys and can be difficult, if not impossible, for a layperson to comprehend. If your governing documents are difficult to read, it would be well worth the board's time to consult an attorney for the purpose of creating an executive summary of the responsibilities laid out in them. The summary should be written in plain English.

Often when a board takes a close look at the rules, it discovers that its practice varies significantly from the responsibilities laid out in its governing documents. It isn't easy to enforce rules on neighbors, and over time boards can tend to look the other way when some members violate the rules, especially friends.

In a later chapter, we will go into more detail on rules and their enforcement. For now, we simply want to point out that a careful look at your governing documents can provide an opportunity to implement a new vision for your board. Do you want to change your board practice to come into line with the governing documents, or do you want to change the governing documents to match the practices of your HOA?

Whatever you decide, it is important to make sure that your practice matches the rules laid down. Sometimes, HOA boards can get themselves into real hot water with their members when they attempt to enforce property rights restrictions that are not allowed by their governing documents or when they enforce rules on some members but let other favored members skate by. Such behavior is a recipe for trouble. For one, it creates dissatisfaction among the members. Also, courts tend to look poorly on a board that doesn't follow its own written rules. If a board wants to effectively manage its affairs, it must understand the role and responsibilities given to it by the governing documents, and it must conduct itself accordingly.

What Is Not Your Job

In our work, we see countless HOA boards that find themselves doing the daily work of an HOA. They pick up the trash, do the books (or don't do them), and write citations for those who violate the HOA rules. As important as these activities may be, we believe there are several reasons these are not the responsibility of the board, no matter how small your HOA.

- **Enforcing Rules.** As we've already said, the vast majority of HOAs are too small for neighbors to be enforcing rules on neighbors. If one of the jobs of an HOA is to foster a sense of community among its members, a rules regime administered personally by the board is a recipe for discord and factions. Instead of the board becoming a source of camaraderie and vision, the board is seen by its own members as a punitive organization, like the police.

- **The Daily Work.** Picking up trash and talking to noisy neighbors are tasks that should be handled by all members of an HOA. There is a tendency for the members of any organization to lean back onto the leadership and expect them to carry the load. In an HOA, this tendency is reinforced if the board makes it its job to pick up the trash or mediate disputes between neighbors. HOAs run best when the members see themselves as part of a community working together for common goals. Boards that take on too many of the daily tasks in an HOA undermine this sense of teamwork and instead set themselves up as the parties responsible to keep the boat afloat. This leads to tired and frustrated board members, and residents who take for granted their personal responsibilities to the community.

- **Jobs That Can Be Done by Others.** Boards that grasp their financial and leadership responsibilities have enough on their plates without doing the work that others should do. When a board finally understands the scope of its financial and oversight responsibilities, there really is little time left for managing the daily affairs. A well-run board assigns other people to make sure the light bulbs get changed in the common areas and then stays busy making sure the financial house is in order and that it is working to maintain and improve the community spirit and the services offered by the HOA.

Think of it this way—could you imagine the board of a Fortune 500 corporation running around one of its factories picking up trash? How long would the shareholders put up with such a board? Not long, I hope. Corporate boards have much more important things to do with their time than manage the daily activities of the corporation. That is why they hire a CEO and a team to do that for them. The board of an HOA charged with maintaining the services of the HOA and preserving the value of millions of dollars in real estate needs to think in the same fashion.

What Is Your Job

An HOA is a group of homeowners banded together in order to create community, provide services unattainable to individuals, and preserve and protect home values. The HOA board is a group of volunteers charged with administering the homeowner association to accomplish this task. The exact things it does will vary greatly, based on the authority and responsibilities given it by the governing documents. However, no matter what the specifics are, the role of an HOA board member can be divided up into three different categories: maintaining the amenities and common property, financial management and oversight, and providing direction and vision.

Maintain Amenities and Common Property

Many HOAs offer some kind of amenities to their owners, whether that is a pool, a common room, or even a golf course. Many HOAs also have responsibility for some or all of the physical structures within the HOA. The board is responsible to make sure that these structures and amenities are properly maintained and available for the use of residents.

In the short term, this means making sure that the proper contracts are in place to assure that the common room is cleaned, the pool is safe to use, the grass is mowed, and the buildings are maintained. In the long term, this means making sure that the HOA has enough money in reserves to repair and maintain the amenities and structures.

This responsibility for future repairs runs in conflict to the way in which many HOAs think about fees. Many HOA boards believe that it is their responsibility to keep their fees as low as possible. This myth inevitably damages the long-term financial stability and health of an HOA and its members. Eventually deferred maintenance must be handled. Boards that have shorted their reserves for the sake of low fees will be forced to issue large special assessments to make up the shortfall, and these are always damaging to the property values and financial well-being of the members. Special assessments should be avoided whenever possible. The best way to do this is to maintain proper reserves. Thus a board is responsible to charge fees that will sustain the common property and amenities of the HOA long into the future. We will talk more about how to properly assess fees for services in our chapter on budgeting, later in the book. For now, just remember that your job is to maintain the amenities and common property within the HOA.

Provide Financial Oversight

Dovetailing with its responsibility for the common property of the HOA, the board is responsible to manage the overall financial well-being of the organization. As a board member, you are expected to put the well-being of the organization above your own. This is called a fiduciary duty. The fiduciary duties imposed on board members can be divided into two areas, undivided loyalty and reasonable business judgment.

Undivided loyalty means that each board member must act in the best interests of the HOA. For example, a board member should vote for a needed increase in assessments or for needed reserves even though the board member personally can't afford it. They also need to vote for assessments, repairs, or other matters that are necessary for the health of the HOA, even if some members do not agree.

The second fiduciary duty of a board member—reasonable business judgment—requires that each board member understand the HOA's business, actively participate in overseeing the HOA, determine what is required for the HOA to operate, and then vote prudently. For example, the law might not require three proposals on a project. However, it is a reasonable method to determine a fair price to pay for work. It is also reasonable to pay for competent advice when necessary. Engineering, law, accounting, and reserve planning are all areas that require a high level of training to do well. The board is not elected to go it alone but to use prudent judgment based on competent input. While this may cost money, the consequences of uninformed decisions are usually much more expensive.

Prudent management of the financial well-being of an HOA also requires that board members have some basic knowledge of financial reports and be able to read them properly. Without this knowledge, many boards are left at the mercy of management companies and professional managers, some of whom may not have the best interests of the HOA at heart. They may be overcharging for the use of their in-house landscaping staff, or their hourly maintenance rates may be well above standard. Board members need to be able to spot this wasteful spending and correct it. This will require a basic knowledge of how to read financial reports and a willingness to do so before the monthly meeting.

Embezzlement is an all-too-prevalent problem in the world of HOAs. In fact, considering the frequent lack of cash controls, it is a wonder it doesn't happen more often. Prudent judgment requires that boards act to protect their funds from embezzlement by using proper cash controls. We will have more to say on both of these financial topics in a later section of this book.

Provide Direction and Vision

The third and final responsibility of HOA boards is to provide direction for the future. This is perhaps the least tangible of the board's responsibilities, but at times it will be the most important. Boards need to be in touch with their members and understand the culture of their HOA. They need to make decisions based upon the needs and wants of their members. For instance, an HOA with large numbers of families might consider closing down a rarely used common room in favor of expanded park facilities.

Serving on an HOA board often feels discouraging because too many boards spend their time reacting to emergencies rather than proactively tackling needed projects and improving property value for their residents. HOA boards are not meant to act as the police, a fire department, or an HOA EMT service. While a board may be the HOA's first responder in a true emergency, this should not be the primary reason for the board's existence.

A board that takes a proactive, task-oriented approach to managing common property and providing services to an HOA creates a sense of mission and accomplishment among the board members and a stronger sense of community among the HOA's residents. In order to remain vital, HOAs need to have a sense of direction, and it is the board's responsibility to provide it. Whether it is revising the HOA's rules, amending the governing documents, or replacing outdated play equipment, HOA boards function best when they are accomplishing tangible tasks.

Tasks for a board can come in all shapes and sizes, from "can wait" to urgent. To start, we recommend that a board work together to compile a comprehensive list. Once it is created, prioritize the list according to urgency and funding requirements. Make sure you research the cost and implications before you act. For example, deciding to bring all architectural violations into compliance this year could be an enormous and volatile task. Remember, volunteer time and effort will be required, so make sure to allow enough time to get the job done.

One way to do this is to lay out a five-year plan of action. Many of the problems you face have taken years to create. It will take time to undo them. Pace yourself so that you don't wear out your board or your volunteers.

Once you have a five-year plan, it is important that the board bring the community members into the process. We suggest that you hold a special meeting at which you seek feedback. You should expect criticism of the plan and resistance to change. At this point, it is vital that you listen carefully to the concerns of the members and incorporate their feedback into your plan. By taking their concerns to heart, you will help the membership become invested in the outcome.

Having a five-year plan, or at least a list of tasks to be accomplished, will change the budgeting process for many boards. Having specific tasks in mind when creating the budget helps take much of the guesswork out of the process. It is easier to know what to charge for annual assessments when you have goals in mind for the money.

Over time, a task-oriented board can dramatically change the attitude of a flagging HOA. It may not be easy at first. There may be some directors on the board who need to be replaced before a new can-do attitude takes hold. Be patient. Keep focused on the road ahead and not on the potholes in front of you.

Managing Conflicts of Interest

Even if we didn't do so by name, we have already discussed conflicts of interest. Working with undivided loyalty is another name for avoiding conflicts of interest, which are almost inevitable for board members somewhere in their term of service. In almost every case, they will not rise to the level of a violation of the law, but that does not mean they will not damage the HOA, even if technically legal. All sorts of harm can be done to an organization through conflicts of interest, including great financial harm. Every HOA should avoid even the hint of a conflict of interest.

Preventing conflicts of interest on an HOA board needs to take a two-pronged approach. First, every HOA should have rules set in place in the bylaws or resolutions that prohibit situations likely to bring about accusations of conflicts of interest. For instance, all hiring by the board should be done either through a competitive bid process for vendors or through a formal interview process for employees. These kinds of formal procedures help a board avoid accusations of conflicts of interest down the road.

Second, besides having standardized procedures in place, the best policy is for board members to be on the lookout for potential conflicts and err on the side of caution. Conflicts of interest can be quite subtle. A CPA sitting on an HOA board might have a client apply for a landscaping contract. An owner of a preschool might also want to sit on the board of the condominium association that owns the property where the preschool is located. In both of these situations, board members would find themselves with conflicting interests. Especially with the case of the preschool owner, these conflicting interests would certainly warrant that the board member stand aside when matters related to the source of the conflict were discussed. Here, the best defense for any board member is to understand the various interests they serve and make sure they are kept separated, wearing their board member hat when serving the HOA and standing aside when necessary.

The People Factor

An HOA board does its best work when it thinks about itself in a similar fashion to a corporate board of directors. However, HOA boards face several challenges not faced by corporate boards. The "people factor" can make the process of managing an HOA much more difficult than any other form of real estate management. The lines between management (the board) and residents (homeowners) are not rigidly defined. Residents are both neighbors and clients and in an HOA, the owner members have at stake not only a huge portion of their financial well-being, but also their sense of community and home. When managing an office complex, a strip mall, or an apartment, a business owner can be somewhat impersonal when making decisions. In an HOA, the human factor keeps getting in the way of the business decisions. Leading an HOA takes a large dollop of people skills along with financial and business savvy. Not only do HOA board members and managers have to be business people, they also have to be as compassionate as Mother Teresa. They are expected to intuitively "know" when the "business deal" is off and "humanity" is on. It is a tightrope from which even the best will fall at times. It takes finesse and skill to pass a needed special assessment by the members without a revolt.

While we may have laid out the responsibilities of a board member in this chapter, it will take practice and patience to develop the bedside manner that must accompany the position. We will talk more about some practical aspects to managing the relationship between the board and its members in later chapters. However, before we get there, we need to cover one of the most important tools an HOA board has for getting the work done and creating needed distance between board policies and the membership—the professional manager.

Three:
Finding, Hiring, and Overseeing a Great Manager

In the last chapter, we suggested that boards function best when they focus on the oversight and future vision for an HOA—in other words, we believe they should behave like the board of directors from a Fortune 500 company. We can almost hear some of you saying, "but who's going to get the work done?" It's a great question.

The work entailed in managing an HOA varies greatly. A small HOA with little common property may have the odd collection call or rules complaint but little else that requires doing in a given month. On the other end of the spectrum, there are boards that manage golf courses, fitness complexes, swimming pools, and parks, not to mention maintenance on the commonly owned buildings and sometimes the streets, as well. Most HOAs fall somewhere in the middle between these two extremes, as defined by the governing documents of the HOA. (Are you coming to understand why we think it is so important for boards to familiarize themselves with their governing documents?)

We believe strongly that every board, no matter how small, should have some kind of relationship with a professional manager. For the board of a large and complex HOA, this will mean hiring a professional manager solely dedicated to administering its HOA. However, only a few HOAs are complex and large enough to make this a cost-effective choice, so we are not going to spend a lot of time discussing that option. Most HOAs will benefit from hiring a professional management company to help them get the monthly work done.

In this chapter, we want to focus on the relationship between the HOA and the management company. We will lay out our case for why every HOA should have some kind of relationship with a management company or a professional manager. Then we want to look more closely at the process of choosing a management company and a manager. Problems are best solved before they're created, and getting the right team in place for your HOA can make all the difference both in your experience on the board and for your members. Finally, we want to give you a tool that you can use to evaluate the service provided by your current property manager, address problems, and decide when to make a change.

Why Your HOA Needs a Manager

Let's not beat around the bush. Hiring a professional manager feels expensive to many HOA boards. It is a big line item in the budget. We also recognize that some managers have little more experience running an HOA than does the board. However, we still believe it is worth the cost for every HOA board to hire an experienced and qualified manager. Consider the alternative—you. It may be frustrating to deal with a manager at times, but it is better than doing it all yourself. Few HOAs have the volunteers to manage their own affairs in a top-notch manner. Some do all right, but most stumble a lot.

There are several practical reasons even the smallest HOA should have some kind of relationship with a manager.

- **Managers Are Paid.** The concept of "care-free living" promises that someone else will take care of the common property and provide the amenities that I cannot provide for myself. Unless they hire someone else to do the work, the board is that "someone else." Why would a few volunteers work to benefit the many? It's not an appealing calling and may explain why your board has so much trouble finding volunteers.

- **Managers Do Collections.** Strong-arming delinquent neighbors for money is low on most folks' to-do list. Yet to keep the HOA's bills paid, collection has to be done. There are people who do this disagreeable task for a living. They're called managers, and they're pretty good at it, and they don't charge all that much. Chances are, you'll collect more of your money if you use them.

- **Managers Enforce Rules.** Enforcing rules on your neighbors is unpleasant at best and physically threatening at worst. Just try towing a redneck neighbor's junk truck. Do you really need that kind of grief just because you volunteer for the board and believe your HOA should look neat and tidy? A great manager acts as a buffer between the board and the residents. Whereas board members may lose their temper and objectivity when faced with a serious problem, a manager has no ax to grind and can execute a systematic plan to bring offenders back in line. Great managers know how to intervene to help defuse conflict before it escalates.

- **Managers Respond to Emergencies.** HOA business can be a 24/7 affair. Bad news tends to come at night during a rainstorm, a windstorm, or that wild party. If you self-manage, you're on the hook for every call. Believe it or not, management companies offer round-the-clock emergency response, allowing you to go on vacation or get a Friday night out without any worry.

- **Managers Provide Communications.** A great HOA manager provides high quality consistent communication to the residents. No more spending Saturdays folding and delivering newsletters.

- **Managers Oversee Maintenance.** One of the greatest benefits of using a professional manager is consistent maintenance of the property. A property evaluation identifies and prioritizes maintenance needs. Needs that are creating damage are top priority, followed by deferred maintenance, and then long-range capital repairs and replacements (e.g. roofing and painting). By systematically inspecting the property, a management company will take care of little things before they create significant damage. The savings in this category alone can go a long way toward defraying the cost of a manager.

- **Managers Provide Continuity.** Since HOAs are run by volunteer boards, consistency can be a huge problem. Board and committee members come and go. A good manager links these well-meaning volunteer efforts together, filling gaps when volunteerism falls short. He provides a systematic approach to record-keeping, instead of the all-too-frequent box-in-the-coat-closet approach, and provides a consistent expertise in financial management and reporting. A great manager will also help educate new directors on their roles, helping them to maximize their effectiveness.

Most of the time, when a board is dead set against hiring a manager, it has one of several objections. Some boards believe that their HOA is too small and simple to hire a full-time manager. In some instances, that may be the case. However, we believe that even these HOAs need to establish some kind of working relationship with a professional management company, because even the smallest HOA has the occasional delinquent owner, the resident who flouts the rules, or a complex renovation project. A manager on call who can handle these kinds of difficulties can be a highly useful resource.

Sometimes boards have been burned in the past by an incompetent manager who had little or no experience with HOA property management. HOAs are not apartments, and many HOAs make the mistake of hiring a rental property management firm whose primary business is running apartment buildings. Typically, only a few property management companies in a given community have HOA experience. HOA managers need to be familiar with the governing documents and with the state and federal laws affecting HOAs. They need to be willing to understand the specific governing documents for your HOA. Unlike apartment complexes, HOAs cannot be run with a standard set of "rules." A willingness to understand each HOA's needs and philosophy is paramount. Alongside these skills, they also must be patient, diplomatic, respectful, and caring.

We'll talk more about how to find this kind of manager in a few pages. For now, we just want you to recognize that a qualified manager can go a long way toward reducing the board's workload and getting it focused on its oversight and management responsibilities. Before we move on, we need to cover the largest objection to hiring a manager—cost.

Counting the Cost

The number one objection for avoiding help from a professional manager is cost. Yet, as we argued in the last section, using a professional manager is one of the best tools to smooth out the bumps in the road by building a sound foundation of planning, record-keeping, and policy-making. A great manager acts as the board's first responder, handling emergencies so that the board can do its job—management and oversight. Yet the objection remains because the management fee can be one of the largest line items in the HOA's annual budget.

So how is that amount computed? How can HOAs know they are getting value for their dollar? Few management companies have detailed time-reporting systems to calculate costs accurately, but a management company sells its time. The more time spent on your HOA, the greater the cost. The management fee is often a rough estimate based on experience of what it's going to take to manage your account and make a profit.

That fee includes the fixed costs for the management company—like the use of the office copier. There are labor costs including the time needed to handle each account. Then there is that funny notion called "profit." The total fixed costs plus labor and profit margin divided by the total number of units managed yields a company's average charge "per door." The average is between fifteen and thirty dollars per household, per month. Small HOAs may pay more and large ones less per door. Costs will also vary by region.

Considering all the services and expertise that professional management provides, the cost is a bargain. For this fee, the HOA receives proper management of its amenities and common areas. The directors know that the maintenance on the common areas will be handled well. They receive twenty-four-hour emergency service, and they can rest assured that the bookkeeping and finances of their HOA are being handled professionally. Just fifteen to thirty dollars per month is a reasonable burden for the benefits of living the "care free" life of an HOA.

Some of you will object that the monthly cost of a management company is only partially calculated in its per door fee, and this is true. Management companies typically have a fixed monthly management fee based on regular and routine services laid out in the contract. Special services requested by the board carry additional charges. For example, some will include processing insurance claims as part of their fee, while others charge extra. So not all monthly fees are the same, and when picking a management company, boards need to be careful to make sure they understand just what is included in each monthly fee.

Besides the monthly per door charge, all management companies have an hourly rate for extra management charges like special meetings, overseeing large renovation projects, and (often) insurance claims. Maintenance, in particular, is a profit center for a management company. Boards should ask that any extra charges be delineated clearly on their monthly invoices, and they should keep a close eye on these to make sure they are being charged at the contracted rate. That said, management companies often provide handyman-type services that can handle small tasks efficiently.

So what can boards do to minimize these extra costs? There are several ways in which boards can help control these extra management fees.

Reducing Your Management Costs

Typically, a management company will assign a manager to the account. Staff costs are directly related to how many HOAs the manager handles. Managers often spend a lot of time preparing for and following up on board meetings. For a typical board meeting, the manager gathers the information and prepares the management report, reviews the financial statement, attaches relevant correspondence, puts board packets together, and mails or emails them to each director.

Most board meetings are held on weekday evenings at the community, so the manager is required to work after hours and travel, both of which cost the HOA money. (It's built into the contract.) After a meeting, the manager usually has a laundry list of follow-up tasks, which occupy most of the following week. A manager can easily spend from fourteen to twenty hours on board-related business. If a board is willing to flex a little, it can do several things to reduce these costs.

- **Limit Board Meetings to Two Hours.** If expectations are set correctly at the beginning, the agenda will get done. The moral here: less talk, more action.

- **Hold Daytime, Weekday Meetings.** These avoid manager overtime costs.

- **Move Meetings to the Management Office.** This will save manager travel time and mileage expenses.

- **Reduce the Number of Meetings to Four Per Year.** A good budget and management plan should allow the manager to handle most issues with only occasional input from the board.

- **Let the Manager Manage.** Board micro-management duplicates effort and inevitably runs up costs. If your management company is incompetent, get a new one. If qualified, let it do its job. This may be your single biggest cost saver.

- **Make Insurance Claims a Billable Cost.** Insurance claims can take hours of a manager's time. If the management agreement specifically states that insurance claim work is an extra cost to the HOA, then the management company can bill the insurance company for the time it takes to administrate a claim.

- **Bill Delinquent Owners for Collection Costs.** Management time for collecting delinquent assessments should be billed to and recouped from the delinquent owner whenever possible.

- **Charge Owners for Sale Disclosures.** The time a manager spends compiling disclosure information for owner home sales should be charged to the owners.

These are but a few ways that management costs can be trimmed. Be sensitive to your manager's time, and don't pile on unnecessary tasks that ultimately will raise the cost. While it's important to get what you pay for, it's equally important to pay for what you get. Sit down with your management company annually to count the cost and work together to improve your partnership. A board that is willing to go the extra mile to respect a manager's time should be rewarded with better service and lower costs.

Creating a Request for Proposal (RFP)

Finding a great management company and a satisfactory manager isn't easy. It may take several calls to local management companies before you find one that specializes in HOA management. An industrious board might start by calling other local HOAs. Nowadays, some have websites and a phone number. A few quick phone calls to a couple of board presidents can often tell you if they are happy with their managers. If you try to find HOAs that seem similar to yours these calls can give you a picture of which firms have satisfied customers and which don't. It can also give you a sense of their management style. Do they provide timely reports? Do they handle collections effectively? Are they responsive to maintenance requests?

Whatever method you choose, a commitment to the prudent management of your HOA would mean that you keep making these phone calls until you find at least three different management companies who might fit the bill. Once you have three different companies in mind, it is time to send them a request for proposal (RFP). This is where the board really needs to put in some time if it wants to find a good fit for its HOA. Clearly defining the needs of your HOA in the RFP is critical. Otherwise, each company will submit a proposal of its choosing that may or may not fit the HOA. If this happens, how can the board compare them?

On the pages that follow, we have included a sample RFP for you to use as a template when you create your own. Make sure that the details you include conform to the needs of your HOA.

Request for Management Proposal
Nottacare Condominium
123 Easy Street
Anytown, USA

Request for Proposal
You are requested to present a management proposal for our homeowner association based on the criteria set forth below. Please mail your proposal by no later than midnight, _____, 201__ to Board President, 123 Easy Street, Anytown, USA. To preview the property or discuss particular aspects of this management proposal,

call the board president (fill in name) at 333.333.3333. **Please respond immediately if you are not interested in presenting a proposal.**

In your proposal, please include:

- Sample of your management contract
- Monthly charge for routine management tasks
- **For each task listed below, a list of any special/extra charges and when they apply**
- Credentials you and your company have for managing homeowner associations
- List of current client references and board president contact information

Description of Homeowner Association
Nottacare Condominium was built in 1978. The facilities consist of eight residential buildings of eights units each, one clubhouse adjoining the pool, one maintenance storage building, and 1.4 acres of landscaped common area. Governing Documents: set of the recorded Declaration, Bylaws, and Articles of Incorporation is attached.

Operating and Reserve Budget
Copy of the current year's approved Operating and Reserve Budget is attached.

Reserve Study
Attached is a copy of this year's Reserve Study.

Governing Body
A volunteer board of directors consisting of five elected members manages the business of the homeowner association. The members of the board of directors each serve two-year terms, which are staggered, so that two come due in even-numbered years and three in odd-numbered years. If a vacancy occurs, a board appointee fulfills the remaining term of the vacated position. After each annual meeting, the directors decide among themselves who will serve as president, vice president, secretary, and treasurer for the coming year. There are no term limitations.

Board Meetings

Board meetings are held on the third Wednesday of January, April, July, and October to:

- *Review current financial reports*
- *Review delinquencies and approve collection action*
- *Review maintenance concerns*
- *Review rule violations or appeals*
- *Hear concerns and requests from members*
- *Enact rules, regulations, and policies*
- *Otherwise deal with business affecting the homeowner association*

Annual Meeting

An annual meeting is held on the third Wednesday of November of each year. The purposes are to:

- *Provide a discussion forum for members*
- *Provide an overview of the previous year's operations*
- *Review the previous year's financials*
- *Discuss the coming year's plan of operation*
- *Review next year's budget*
- *Discuss and vote on amendments to the bylaws and/or proposed policy*
- *Elect new board members*

Regular Assessments

Regular fees are collected monthly from each member. The board may adjust fees annually to keep pace with known cost increases and the local inflation index, unless such exceeds a 10% increase. Increases over 10% must be voted upon and approved by a simple majority of the members of the association. Regular assessments are payable on the 1st day of each month and are subject to a $25 late charge after the 10th and every 30 days thereafter until paid. All partial payments are applied to the oldest balance first.

Special Assessments

In the event of operating or reserve budget shortfall, the board may request approval by the members of a special assessment. The board has the authority to pass a special assessment.

Accounting Functions
These functions must be performed monthly:

- Collecting money from members, including delinquencies
- Paying bills
- Preparing monthly financial statements on an accrual basis, including:
  - ◦ Income and expense, year-to-date vs. budget statements
  - ◦ A balance sheet
  - ◦ A statement of aging receivables
  - ◦ Copies of the most recent bank statements and a reconciliation report
- Keeping current member data (name, address, contact information)

Maintenance Responsibilities
Manager shall oversee regular maintenance of the buildings and grounds, including but not limited to:

- General repairs
- Gutters and downspout cleaning [ ] monthly or [ ] ___ times per year.
- Painting
- Maintaining common area lighting
- Siding repairs
- Driveway and parking lot sweeping
- Railings, fences, and walls
- General landscaping, sprinkler, and tree maintenance
- Pool maintenance
- Clubhouse maintenance

Enforce Rules, Regulations, and Policies
The homeowner association has a number of rules, regulations, and policies that require enforcement from time to time. Manager is responsible for responding to reports of violations, notifying offenders, and enforcing penalties as outlined in the schedule of fines. (List of rules attached.)

Distribute Information
Manager shall distribute the following information to members:

- *Governing documents*
- *Rules and regulations*
- *Special policies and regulations*
- *Schedule of fines*
- *List of approved service providers*
- *Board and manager contact information*
- *Attend meetings: Manager to attend ____ board meetings per year of no more than two hours each and one annual meeting of no more than two hours.*

At board meetings, manager shall:
- *Give a manager's report of current events since the previous board meeting*
- *Provide and review current financial statements with the board*
- *Advise board on good management practices in dealing with business matters as needed*
- *Alert board to maintenance, collections, rules, or other issues that require board input*
- *Assist in reviewing contract proposals*
- *Distribute meeting minutes prepared by board secretary*

Before and at the annual meeting, manager shall:
- *Assist in preparation and distribution of the notice of annual meeting, agenda and proxy*
- *Arrange for the meeting place*
- *Prepare sign-in sheets, ballots, agendas, and other handouts needed for the meeting*
- *Present a manager's report of the previous year's activity and plans for the coming year*
- *Assist in the election process*

Newsletter Preparation
Manager shall produce and distribute a newsletter by the first day of February, May, August, and November, which includes:

- *Most recent board meeting minutes*
- *Most current income and expense statement (year-to-date vs. budget)*
- *Community news*
- *Commonly violated rules reminder*
- *Event calendar (maintenance, meetings, and social)*

- *Major renovation schedule*
- *Board and manager contact information*
- *Other information the board wants included*

General Scope of Board Authority
The board oversees all business of the homeowner association. The board president is authorized to give specific direction to the manager as defined by a written management contract executed by both parties. The board approves all new policy and rules. The board president has authority between board meetings to act on emergency, non-routine matters that cannot wait for a scheduled board meeting. Non-emergency issues will be handled at regular board meetings. The board may appoint committees to oversee significant issues.

General Scope of Committee Authority
The board-appointed committees include Landscaping, Rules, Maintenance, and Budget. Committee chairs may give manager specific direction on routine matters relating to the committee function.

General Scope of Manager Authority
The manager has the authority to:

- *Execute normal and routine business on behalf of the association that is in keeping with the governing documents, state statutes, and the approved budget*
- *Respond to emergencies such as fires, floods, and other situations that threaten residents and/or common property*
- *Pay all routine bills. Pay non-budgeted expenses that do not exceed $500. Other bills may need either board president or board approval based on the amount prior to payment. All checks relating to reserve expenses must be signed by both board president and treasurer*
- *Enforce collection of delinquencies according to a board-approved collection policy*
- *Enforce rules and fines defined in written board policies*
- *Enforce all other written board policies*
- *Schedule repairs and maintenance that is in keeping with the approved operating budget*
- *Respond to routine information and maintenance requests from members*

- *Gather proposals for routine service contracts*
- *Maintain a records system that may be accessed during business hours by association members*
- *Coordinate insurance claims and related repairs*
- *Provide management recommendations to the board when advisable*
- *Perform other tasks as authorized by the board president*
- *Provide resale disclosure information to sellers who request it. Indicate if additional fee will be charged: $_____*

Before the Interviews

Once the proposals come in, the hard work of sorting through them begins. Hopefully, since you used an RFP similar to the one in the previous section, each proposal will address the costs for the specific tasks required to keep your HOA up and running smoothly. With a little work, you should be able to make an apples-to-apples comparison between them.

In our experience, it is vital that board members review the sample contract provided by the management firm. As they say, the devil is in the details. When it comes to contracts, it's always prudent to hire a knowledgeable attorney. Here is a list of questions to consider when reviewing a sample contract provided by a management company:

- **Does the contract contain termination fees?** Most management company contracts have termination clauses that require several months' notice. Unless there is a serious breach of contract, like embezzlement, this kind of requirement is reasonable. Switching to a new management company is a complex undertaking and the manager will want plenty of time for information transfer. You should not, however, agree to pay a "special termination fee."

- **Does the contract work well with our HOA's needs and philosophy?** The contract you sign should be tailored to fit the specific needs of your HOA. While the contract you review is a draft, and can be altered significantly once the management firm has a better understanding of your needs, the board should be able to get a good idea of whether its HOA will fit well with the management style of the company.

- **How are the costs structured?** HOA boards need to make sure that costs are transparent and not structured to hit the board with unexpected bills down the road. An all-too-common strategy some management companies use to get your business is to offer a cut-rate monthly fee for basic services and then charge a high hourly rate for everything else not specifically itemized in the basic monthly amounts. Some proposals will look cheap but may well be much more expensive when all the additional fees are added together. Some will also give greater leeway for the management company to charge by the hour for work. If it charges by the hour for services you will often use, this may be an expensive proposition for the board.

- **Does the contract contain clauses that require or create incentives to use management company vendors?** Another tactic that some management companies use to increase their profits are kickback fees from vendors. Management companies often have a list of approved vendors. Those accepting a fee for being listed or any other form of compensation are violating their fiduciary duties to their HOAs. Of course, few if any will disclose such arrangements. One way to vet the issue is to create a provision in the management agreement that states the management company or manager is not allowed to accept any compensation from vendors doing work for the HOA.

Interviewing Management Companies

Once the board has sorted through the proposals, and it has an idea which companies might fit the HOA, the board should then set up an interview with the specific manager at the management company who will be assigned to the HOA. Remember, the manager will, for all intents and purposes, be the face of the board to its members. It is vital to the interests of the board and the members that the manager handles all in a professional manner. It may be the case that everything looks great on paper but the actual manager may turn out to be a cold fish.

Be careful to make sure your interview is with the specific manager who will be assigned to your HOA. We have seen cases where a top-quality manager is sent out to the interview, only to have the HOA assigned a different manager once the ink on the contract is dry. If the manager is going to be the face of your HOA to your members and to the public, don't you think you ought to get to interview them before you hire them?

The questions you ask at the interview should be designed to establish three things. First, they should establish that the board is comfortable with the management firm as a whole and its practices. Second, they should make sure that the board is comfortable with the individual who will be assigned to manage the HOA. Finally, the questions should reassure the board that the management company uses financial procedures that are transparent and set up to minimize the possibility of embezzlement. Here is a list of the kinds of questions we recommend HOA boards ask every management company:

General Questions:

- Do you have any questions regarding the proposal (e.g. the number of newsletters prepared, etc.)?
- How many HOAs does each manager handle?
- Are there multiple departments handling the work or does the assigned manager do all the tasks?
- What services are handled in-house, and what are hired out to vendors?
- On what basis are the financial statements kept? [Do not hire a management firm that uses cash-basis accounting. We will explain why in a later chapter.]
- What are the procedures for assigning a new manager if our current manager leaves during the contract?

Questions for the Property Manager Who Will Be Assigned to the HOA:

- Do you hold any specific credentials for HOA management?
- How many HOAs do you manage?
- How long have you been an HOA manager?

- Tell us about a time you handled a very difficult collection and were successful.
- Give us a specific example of how you handled a major rules violation and the results.
- What part of your job do you like the least?
- Can you provide us with three references from HOAs you manage?

Questions to Help Prevent Embezzlement:

- Do you pool client money in one bank account or does every client have its own bank accounts for operating and reserve funds?
- Who will have check-writing authority on our operating account?
- Are you comfortable if we get copies of all bank statements for every account sent directly to us?
- Are those who handle our cash bonded? What is the bond amount you carry and is it shared with multiple clients?
- Has anyone in your management company ever been accused of embezzlement?

Evaluating Proposals and Interviews

Sorting through the information returned to the board in a proposal can be a time-consuming task. Below we've included a checklist that can help boards create a comparison that makes sense. Like our sample RFP in the previous section, this checklist will be a much more powerful tool if it is adapted to the specific needs of your association.

Management Screening Checklist

Date:_____, 20___
Company:_____
Contact:_____Title:_____
Address:_____
City:_____State_____Zip_____
Phone:_____ Fax: _____ Cell:_____
Email:_____Website:_____

☐   *Meetings: Attends ____ board meetings per year plus one annual homeowner meeting, all included in the basic management fee. Additional meetings carry a charge of $_____*

☐   *Meeting Notices: Will prepare and distribute meeting notices and agendas as directed by the board president. Will also assist with procedure at these meetings.*

☐   *Property Inspections: Performs general grounds and buildings inspection and follows up on any needed maintenance or problems at least: ☐ Weekly ☐ Monthly ☐ Quarterly*

Maintenance Services

☐   *Maintenance Scheduling: Orders maintenance on the buildings and grounds, according to standard practice or as directed by the board president, and follows up to ensure completion. Prepares schedules of regular and extraordinary maintenance and repairs.*

☐   *Provides handyman maintenance services at $___/hour during business hours, $___/hour after hours, $___/hour on holidays.*

☐   *Performs larger renovation projects like painting, siding, and deck repair, etc., on a: ☐ bid/proposal basis ☐ time and material basis.*

☐   *Major Repair Projects: Assists in the specifications, bid proposals, and project oversight of major repairs. Included in the basic management fee or for an extra charge of: $_____*

☐   *Emergency Response: Maintains a 24-hour emergency response service.*

☐ *Purchases: Negotiates contracts for services, tools, equipment, materials, and supplies for the operation and maintenance of the association's property.*

☐ *Insurance Claims: Processes association insurance claims for: ☐ No extra charge ☐ An extra fee that will be included with the claim.*

☐ *Relations with Owners: Responds to owner information, maintenance, or service requests, and records action taken.*

Financial Responsibilities:

☐ *Collects, records, and deposits assessments to association's bank account in a timely manner.*

☐ *Pays bills as authorized by the board in a timely fashion.*

☐ *Prepares monthly income & expense statements, balance sheet, and delinquency report in a format usable by the board and auditors. Arranges for audit as directed by board.*

☐ *Maintains bank accounts and provides monthly financial statements.*

☐ *Sends delinquency notices, levies fines, processes liens, and initiates legal action against delinquent owners in accordance with the association collection policy.*

☐ *Sale Documentation: Provides sale disclosure information as requested by seller for a cost of $_____. Billed to seller or HOA?_____*

☐ *Directory: Maintains current directory of owners/residents, addresses, phone numbers, and email addresses.*

☐ *Files & Records: Maintains current financial, maintenance, and administrative records in an orderly fashion and readily accessible by authorized association representatives.*

☐   *Insurance: Arranges insurance as indicated by the governing documents or as directed by the board.*

☐   *Annual Budget: Prepares draft annual budget for board review.*

☐   *Reserve Study: Assists the board or a reserve analyst in the review and update of the association reserve study.*

Other: _____

Other: _____

Monthly Management Fee $ _____

Evaluation of the Company Proposal: Excellent Average Poor

Evaluation of the Manager Interview: Excellent Average Poor

Overall Evaluation: Excellent Average Poor

Negotiating the Contract

Once you have interviewed at least three different management companies and followed up on the references, it is time to look seriously at the contract that you are about to sign. Too often HOA boards treat a proposed contract like a finished product and simply sign it. This won't do, unless the board is truly satisfied with the terms. The HOA board should have an attorney look over the contract to evaluate its terms and suggest language that will protect the HOA's interests. Only after the contract has been negotiated to each party's satisfaction can the board make a decision to go forward with signing the agreement.

Evaluating Your Manager

When an HOA hires a management company, it should expect the manager to handle its affairs in a professional manner. We believe there are certain habits and behaviors that make some HOA managers much more effective than others. The following eighteen key indicators touch on areas of a manager's job that make or break his or her effectiveness.

1. Communicates openly and honestly with the board
2. Responds to information and maintenance requests promptly
3. Is reasonably accessible by phone and email
4. Is prepared for board and owner meetings
5. Vigorously pursues delinquent homeowner fees
6. Produces complete, readable, and timely financial reports
7. Obtains at least three qualified proposals for large renovation projects
8. Regularly attends HOA continuing education programs
9. Is knowledgeable about construction and maintenance management
10. Spends funds prudently without sacrificing quality and workmanship
11. Uses only licensed, bonded, and insured service providers
12. Consistently acts with the HOA's best interests in mind
13. Has a good understanding of HOA governing documents
14. Has a proactive management style
15. Avoids conflicts of interest with vendors or maintenance providers
16. Avoids profiting from service providers' services
17. Brings to the HOA the benefits of volume purchasing
18. Is a specialist in HOA management

Out of a total of eighteen, how did your manager do? Managers who score fifteen to eighteen should be valued. If you have one, hang on for dear life. If your manager didn't score above fourteen, then sit down with them and discuss your concerns in a professional manner.

Of course, good manager-board relations are clearly more complicated than a simple checklist, but if your manager scored below nine, be open to the possibility that it may be time for a needed change. Chances are that you have already heard complaints from your members about the manager's attitude. You may have noticed maintenance isn't completed on time, is done in a shoddy manner, or both. Site inspections may be infrequent. Phone calls aren't returned promptly, and collections or rules violations are left unresolved.

Hopefully, if you used our process for choosing a management company, your agreement should be detailed enough so that both the board and the manager understand what is expected. The board is of course entitled to expect professional performance of the services listed in the contract. On the other hand, the manager is entitled to expect that the scope of work is limited to that listed in the contract. There is plenty to do with routine tasks, and managers that aren't careful about the kinds of services offered will soon become overwhelmed.

When it comes to complaints about collections or fines, the board needs to be careful. If the manager is following the established policy and is respectful in the execution, then getting complaints just runs with the territory. However, if the manager is being overbearing or rude, that's another issue. Boards need to understand the basis of the complaints received. The manager has a right to expect that the board will support him or her with difficult tasks. On the other hand the board has the right to expect professional conduct. Are the complaints widespread and specific? If most of the residents are up in arms, there is probably something to worry about.

Another source of complaints about manager performance is how soon maintenance gets done. The manager's job is to manage HOA maintenance efficiently and cost-effectively. This requires that small jobs accumulate, and turn-around may take several weeks or longer. Most HOA's can't afford to do otherwise. So, unless it's an emergency, residents need to be patient.

Then there are delays in newsletters and financial statements. Here we strongly believe these should be calendared in the contract. Other correspondence can be handled with more flexibility. For example, it's not unusual for lenders and title companies to place an urgent phone call on the day of a home closing, demanding more documentation. The manager should not feel obligated on account of this poor planning on the part of others and can't drop everything to respond. The board should also recognize that the manager is often juggling requests from several HOAs at any given moment in time. Many managers want to please, but there is only so much time in a day. If, however, a manager has committed to a deadline and is consistently missing it, there is a problem that the board should discuss with her or him.

If the time comes when frustration with a particular manager is reaching critical mass, go slowly. All HOA managers and management companies have strengths and weaknesses, so moving to another company may not solve your problem and may actually make problems worse. A visit to the management company office might be just the ticket you need to figure out if your manager is the problem or if the problems are systemic to the company itself. If you believe that the problem lies with your particular manager, see if you can change to a different manager within the same firm before starting to hunt for a new company altogether.

In the end, the board and manager should always work as a team. The board adopts rules, enacts policy, and approves the budget. The manager executes the board's plan in conjunction with the governing documents and state and federal law. Communication should be clear and frequent. Dealing with small issues before they become large will prevent them from escalating into a crisis.

Four: Communication Is the Key to Keeping Members Happy

It is hard to overestimate the value of relevant, timely communication with your members. It really doesn't matter how well your board has performed in the last year if your members haven't been told. Where information is lacking, rumors often fill the gap. When big changes arrive with little or no warning, rebellion often follows. There is perhaps no more important skill set for a proactive board than good communication with its members.

Sometimes HOA boards—along with politicians, corporate directors, and other leaders—believe that since they've been elected, their members will automatically trust and approve of all their decisions. It's easy to get busy doing the right thing and forget to communicate with your membership. Next thing you know, the rumor mill is running at full capacity, and extra effort must be taken to convince your members that you did the right thing.

We believe that the best communication strategies are proactive. Regular newsletters, proper signage, and a forum to vent grievances are all tools that forward-thinking boards deploy to make sure they hear their members' concerns and communicate effectively. Proactive communication lets a board know whether it is on track or derailed with its members. As the saying goes, "The light at the end of the tunnel may be the headlight of an oncoming train." Better to know sooner than later.

On the other hand, reactive communication systems keep the board on the defensive and are indicative of a crisis-based management style. Here nothing gets communicated unless the smell of tar and feathers is in the air.

Good communication isn't simply about avoiding problems, either. Good communication fosters community and creates an environment in which neighbors feel invested in the HOA. The board that makes its decisions behind closed doors with little input from the homeowners will find it difficult to recruit new board members and volunteers when needed. Frequent, honest, and upbeat communication is a key tool to creating an HOA where community thrives and the care-free lifestyle is a reality.

It Starts With Listening

While proactive communication from the board is an important piece of the puzzle for any HOA, good communication starts elsewhere. It starts with listening. There's an old saying, "God gave you one mouth and two ears for a reason." HOA board members must master the art of knowing when to speak and when to listen. The greater skill is the ability to listen.

Boards and managers deal with irate homeowners on a regular basis. Their intensity, irrational fears, and disrespectful behavior can make the blood boil. The urge to strike back is natural.

It can be hard to remember that the person yelling at you is a shareholder in the HOA who believes passionately in their cause. As a shareholder, that person is owed a full and fair hearing. As a leader and representative of the board, your role is to stay calm, listen attentively, and, if possible, discover the key to the conflict before you take action.

Effective listening is the key to dealing with difficult personalities in your community. Listening without interrupting or jumping to conclusions can be mastered by even the most type-A personality. Listening means really concentrating on what the other person is saying and not simply waiting for your turn to speak. Listen with both eyes and ears. Keep an open posture with arms at your sides, instead of crossed in front of you, which indicates defensiveness. Let your body language show that the person speaking has your full and undivided attention. Show that you care about their concerns.

While the issue under discussion may be emotionally charged, the effective listener focuses on the facts, not the emotion. A great listener spends their time trying to understand the specifics of the problem, including the actions the speaker would like the board to take and why it is being brought to the board's attention.

After a frustrated person has expressed their concerns, an effective listener can often calm them by restating key elements in the conversation and asking whether they have understood correctly. This is more than simply some form of psychobabble. Echoing back the key elements of the conversation and allowing the speaker to agree to them sets a foundation for future conversations, in which the speaker feels heard and respected, even if in the end you do not agree with them.

When you finally do get a turn to speak, make sure you don't damage the foundation of good will you've created through listening by now using inflammatory language. Express your opinions as your own. Focus on speaking about the problem at hand, not the person bringing the complaint. Of course, there are situations where no amount of diplomacy will win the day. There are times when you can listen all you want to no avail. In these instances, it may be better to try again after a reasonable cooling-off period.

Diplomacy

In the end, what we are talking about is good diplomacy. In an HOA, good diplomacy on the part of the board can make the difference between friendly resolution and a lawsuit. Here are ten questions you can ask yourself to make sure that you are valuing the good of the community over being right or winning an argument.

1. Can you communicate clearly that your thoughts are opinions, not facts?
2. Do you avoid confrontation with those you're most inclined to argue with?
3. Do you hear the other person out before formulating a reply?
4. Can you find common ground with another person's position?
5. Can you reinforce your views with facts, instead of raw emotion?
6. Do you avoid making sarcastic remarks?
7. Can you keep your cool under fire?
8. Do you truly believe that everyone is entitled to their own opinion?
9. Do you take pride in the battles that you successfully avoided?
10. Do you think others may offer a better solution than yours?

Successful HOA diplomats can answer a firm "yes" to at least seven of these ten questions. If you answered "no" to four or more, perhaps it's time to focus your attention on doing better. Standing up for what you believe in can be a great trait in many situations, but when it gets in the way of your community's progress, it might be better to lose the battle and win the war.

Handling Easily Frustrated People

There's at least one in every HOA—a person who details every infraction, real or imagined. These people find the cloud behind every silver lining and damage the community at every turn. As members, they can't be barred from meetings, but much can be done to defuse their explosive personalities:

- **Let Them Speak Their Minds.** Open forums before important meetings are important tools for calming emotions. Venting helps.

- **Hear Them Out Without Interruption.**

- **Don't Play Favorites.** Allow equal time to all speakers.

- **Keep Cool.** Don't respond to yelling or accusations.

- **Show Concern.** "I understand you are upset...."

- **Consider Their Point Carefully.** Difficult people often challenge the status quo, and they may just be right. Think before giving an automatic "no."

- **Roll Back the Rules.** Rules born of common sense are less subject to challenge. Eliminate those that aren't.

- **Present a United Front.** Decide in advance how to respond to explosive people. When the unified message is "Your behavior is inappropriate, and we're all in agreement on this," the challenge will fail. If the rest of the board sits and squirms, the challenge will prevail.

- **Move Meeting Times Earlier.** Everyone is fresher and more relaxed before the end of a long day.

Sometimes there will be no going around these problem members. However, using these techniques can go a long way to defusing any trouble. Treating problem members with respect, especially in public meetings, also sends a signal to the other members of the HOA that the board will consider all opinions. That simple act will go a long way toward making sure the problem person is taken with a large grain of salt when complaining to other members. Consider respect toward those who may not have earned it as a vaccine against a spreading virus.

So What Do You Tell Your Members?

In the first few sections of this chapter, we've talked about how to listen well as a board in order to defuse problems and keep them from escalating. Now we need to turn our attention to the other side of the coin—what message you should present to your members and how to make sure it's effectively heard.

HOAs obligate their members to the association, and their neighbors, both financially and otherwise. HOAs have an obligation to their members to make clear just exactly what these obligations entail. Many states have disclosure requirements when a buyer purchases a home in an HOA. Others do not. However, we believe that all HOAs, whether obligated by the law or not, should conduct their affairs in an open manner. Here is a list of documents that we believe should be available to members upon request:

- **Governing Documents.** Includes the Declaration, Bylaws, Rules & Regulations, and Resolutions that are the specific obligations each member has to the HOA and other residents.

- **Newsletters.** Reveal events (renovation, litigation, etc.) that could indicate a possible special assessment.

- **Meeting Minutes.** Same as newsletter but with more specifics.

- **Annual Budgets for Last Three Years.** Could reveal expense trends and failure to adjust for inflation.

- **Financial Reports.** Monthly reports comparing actual expenses to budget should be available to track income and expenses.

- **Collection Activity.** How much of the assessments are overdue thirty, sixty or ninety days? If some don't pay, guess who gets to?

- **Litigation Activity.** Are there any pending lawsuits that could trigger a special assessment?

- **Reserve Study.** A thirty-year plan for HOA-maintained components like roofs, painting, paving, etc. A missing reserve study is the biggest time bomb for many HOAs. Failure to plan for predictable long-range expenses often mirrors a lack of ongoing maintenance, which causes downward spiraling property values.

- **Key Contact Information.** How to contact the board and manager.

Beyond making these basic documents available to members, boards also need to make sure that members are well aware of any changes to fees likely to come their way. We will have a whole chapter on how to communicate about special assessments, and a section in our chapter about budgeting deals with the specific steps an HOA can take to communicate about proposed fees. The best way to head off trouble is to stay in front of it by communicating about it with members, long before a board meeting or the annual meeting. Boards who want to keep rebellion to a minimum take great care to make sure their members don't experience any surprises when the board makes a tough decision.

Eight Great Ways to Share the Good News

Reliable and accurate communication systems are a must for HOAs that want to avoid reacting to crisis and stay proactive. It's also essential that they set up systems that allow their members to provide feedback and suggestions. Here are eight great ways to communicate with your members:

1. **The Internet.** Bar none, the Internet is the fastest and cheapest way to interact with the membership. Most folks now have email addresses, so why continue to waste time and money on copies, labels, stamps, envelopes, and the US Snail Service if you don't need to? For about $1/day, your HOA can have its own website with key information posted and a turbo-charged communication system.

2. **Newsletters.** These can be as small as one page and as large as the *LA Times*, depending on how much time, budget, volunteer effort, and information there is. Pick a format and catchy name, and stick with it. Make the information interesting. Decide at budget time how many newsletters there will be and when they will be produced. And rather than print them, use PDF and email them. For more newsletter basics, go to www.Regenesis.net.

3. **Flyer Boxes.** Flyers distributed at the mailbox, clubhouse, and other common points are a quick and cheap way to get the word out. Don't forget to mail to non-resident members.

4. **Message Board.** Very effective if properly located and managed. Don't let messages stay for more than a week, as they blend into the landscape. Keep the board neat and sectioned according to topic.

5. **Member Forum.** Always give the members a voice at board meetings by way of a pre-meeting Member Forum designed to let them speak their mind, ask questions, or offer suggestions. To facilitate this, always hold your meetings in a location that is large enough to accommodate guests.

6. **Automated Phone Trees.** There are great options available on the Internet that allow you to communicate a voice message to a list of phone numbers. See www.voiceshot.com, www.call-em-all.com, www.onecallnow.com, and others.

7. **Welcome Packets.** These can include things like the governing documents, budgets, rules and regulations, and other need-to-know information. The message should be, as the name implies, "Welcome to the neighborhood!" Include architectural guidelines, maps, clubhouse and pool schedules, and management and emergency contact information. To save paper, put all this information on a website, which can be updated as needed.

8. **HOA Phone Number.** This essential tool is often overlooked. Since board members and managers change, why not have a permanent phone number with voice mail that will alert the right party?

Newsletters

Not all communication from the board in an HOA should be about money. The board exists not only to manage the affairs of the HOA, but also to foster and develop a sense of community among the owners. Newsletters can be a great way to get this done. They provide a way to enlighten, inform, remind, and encourage. Frequent reminders of important rules or architectural policies help build a friendlier and more harmonious community. Recognizing volunteers encourages others to step up. Newsletters needn't be long and involved, just relevant.

Here are some tips designed to help make your newsletter successful:

- **Focus on Building Community.** Get HOA members to become participants, rather than observers. Offer opportunities to do that on committees and social events.

- **Understand Your Audience.** How old are they? What is their financial status? How do they like to spend their time? Find out by getting feedback from your readers with a questionnaire.

- **Inspire Your Readers.** Make sure events, activities and volunteer opportunities are well publicized. Create headlines to grab the reader's attention.

- **Be Consistent in Layout and Content.** If you have a "Rules & Regs Corner" which highlights a particular HOA rule or policy, publish it in every issue. Always include current board and management contact information (mail, email, and phone).

- **Dash the Draft.** Write the rough draft as quickly as possible, then go back to polish and flesh out the details.

- **Archive Your Newsletters and Articles.** Many articles bear repeating, and as time passes, will have eyes that see them for the first time. Repeat seasonal reminders. Create folders on your computer for the months you publish your newsletter, and put article files in the months they fit best. In time, you can build a reservoir of content to draw upon that will make newsletter writing much simpler and quicker.

- **Lead with Your Strong Suit.** Put the most important information up front. Organize the strongest points of an article before you write it.

- **Keep Articles Short.** If an article is long or complicated, readers will move on. If there is simply too much good content to abbreviate, break the article into several articles.

- **Give Credit & Contact Information.** Include the newsletter committee, writer, and editor names and contact information.

- **Be Positive & Uplifting.** While criticism has its place, too much of it is a downer and chases most readers away. Strive for the positive. Be upbeat.

- **Proofread.** Editing is a rewording experience. Carefully review your work for grammatical and spelling mistakes, or get a detail-oriented person to do it for you. Make sure your facts are straight.

- **Reprint with Permission.** Search the Internet for content that would be of interest to your readers. If you find an article that includes author and contact information, be sure to get permission before reprinting and give credit where credit is due.

- **Have Fun with It.** Give them a giggle or two. The Internet is full of jokes, puns, and cartoons.

- **Publish Pictures.** Folks love to see themselves in the paper. Share event pictures, photos of board members, the manager, committee members, and other volunteers.

- **PDF It.** Programs like Adobe Acrobat make it possible to convert word-processing and newsletter documents into Portable Document Format (PDF), which can be posted on the HOA website or emailed to those that do email. You could say that PDF was designed with HOAs in mind. Using it can save thousands of dollars in printing, supplies, and postage each year, plus the countless processing hours required of paper newsletters.

- **Get Advertisers.** If your community is large enough and the newsletter is regular, it may attract advertisers like real estate agents, insurance agents, painters, and remodelers, and help pay for itself.

Five:
Better Meetings

It's no understatement to say that how the board runs its meetings can make or break an HOA. A consistent habit of poorly run meetings can break down all sense of community and leave in its wake disgruntled and disillusioned members. The good news is that it only takes a few new habits for a board to give its meetings a new, constructive feel.

Place and Setting

To start, different meetings demand different settings. HOAs hold both board meetings and member meetings, including the annual meeting. Each of these types of meetings has a unique purpose and outcome and so should be handled in a different fashion.

Board meetings are designed to transact regular business for the care and welfare of millions of dollars of community assets. As such, they should be held at places and times conducive to business. While we recognize home board meetings will happen, they can be challenging to pull off well, and we advise against them if at all possible.

HOA members are entitled to attend all board meetings—as an audience, not as participants in the discussion or in the voting. Board meetings need to provide adequate seating for them. When held in a small home, there is only room for the board. Guests can feel shut out and unwelcome. If a meeting must take place in a home, choose the most spacious setting possible.

Living rooms should be avoided except for guest seating, as it is nearly impossible to pass paperwork and take notes when seated in a recliner. Meetings should be held at a large table where agendas, reports, and other paper can be spread out among the board without the need to continuously shuffle the stack. Cell phones and landlines should be turned off, as they distract from discussion.

The board chair should sit at the head of the table, the traditional place of authority. Guests should *not* be allowed to sit at the table with the board, as this invites their participation in the discussion. If possible, the board should avoid facing the guests as if they were a panel, as this also invites participation.

Ideally, board meetings should be held at a location designed for meetings. Basics would include a large conference table, good lighting, bathrooms, temperature controls, and room for guests. If your HOA doesn't have such a room, seek out meeting rooms in your local community. Churches, libraries, and community centers are ideal locations. They may be closer and less expensive than you would suppose.

Besides eliminating distractions, such locations set the proper tone for the board meeting, keeping the business of the board front and center. Such formality helps avoid the gossip and lingering that can detract from a board meeting. As with homes, such formal settings should have adequate seating for both the board and guests—board at the conference table, guests to the side.

Annual meetings offer their own challenges, and our next section will go into further detail on how to build a strong sense of community through your annual meeting. For now, it is worth pointing out that such meetings should always be held in a formal meeting facility large enough to accommodate all the owners. The board should again be separated from the members up front at a U-shaped table if possible, so that all board members can hear each other. It also helps to keep the meeting from becoming a question and answer session, with the board members on the "firing line." Finally, make sure to have a proper sound system, so that even those at the back can easily hear.

Meeting location and set-up is critical for getting things done efficiently. Set your sights high, and don't forget to check your weapons at the door.

Ground Rules

Productive meetings don't happen by chance. Setting and location can go a long way to keeping them on target, but even the best preparation can fail without proper ground rules. Without ground rules, small issues become major time-wasters, and important matters do not receive the attention they deserve. Ground rules discourage someone from monopolizing the meeting with personal concerns.

One of the best-known guidelines for meetings is Robert's Rules of Order. In some formal settings, like Congress, Robert's Rules are used extensively. We recommend that HOAs follow an abbreviated version. Here are six rules for HOA meetings:

1. One person speaks at a time.

2. The chair decides who that person will be.

3. The speaker may only speak on the issue under consideration.

4. All those wishing to speak will have an opportunity.

5. Decisions require a motion, a second, and a vote.

6. Once the issue is voted upon, no further discussion is permitted.

Requiring that everyone follow the ground rules for a successful meeting is essential to making sure that the HOA functions properly. It is up to the chair to make sure that the rules exist and that they are enforced with diplomacy and fairness.

Board Meetings Are About Getting Things Done

Board meetings are held to transact HOA business. Often this isn't how it works. Some view board meetings as an opportunity to debate and gossip endlessly. This may be interesting to a few, but it drags the board back toward the micro-managing we recommend it avoid. Here are some principles that will help guide your meetings toward success and away from endless debate.

• **Schedule Meetings in Advance.** There is no reason that board meetings can't be scheduled a year in advance. Scheduling meetings far in advance sets deadlines for accomplishment. It defines points in time where decisions will be made at predictable intervals, rather than on the fly. Planning far in advance eliminates the excuse that someone is already booked. It also gives the members the impression that the board is steering the HOA ship instead of being keelhauled underneath it.

- **Create an Agenda.** Every meeting should have an action agenda. An action agenda provides a meeting roadmap. It tells everyone where they are going and what the final destination will be. Without an agenda, any topic is fair game. While it's conceivable that every topic might be of value to the HOA, the ability to make decisions and act is especially limited where there is a lack of preparation. An agenda is critical for staying on course.

- **Plan for Action, Not Debate.** An action agenda calls—as the title implies—for decisions. Instead of "Discuss Landscape Contract," try "Approve Landscape Contract," which implies action. Use the same concept for all agenda items.

- **Distribute the Agenda in Advance.** An action agenda should be distributed in advance and should include supporting information and recommendations for decisions. In other words, "The committee recommends that the plan be adopted as presented." Again, this approach points to decisions, not discussion. All of this should be distributed three to seven days in advance. Keep supporting information as brief and to the point as possible. No one wants to wade through piles of files.

- **Time Limit Your Meetings.** Board members and homeowners have full lives. Endless meetings are a real turn-off. They usually happen because there is no agenda to begin with, and discussion is allowed to meander aimlessly. Agree that meetings will not last longer than two hours and that all agenda items need to be covered during that time. Keep your promise. It's up to the chair to move things along. If your meetings tend to drone on, use a kitchen timer that "dings!" when the time limit has run out on each agenda item.

- **Follow Meeting Protocol.** Unstructured meetings will often deteriorate into chaos if there are no rules to guide the discussion and decision-making, as we said in the last section. But what good are rules if you don't follow them? It's up to the chair to make sure that the meeting runs according to the protocols set by the board. Above all, follow this cardinal rule: Unless at least two people are interested in discussing a topic, move on. If one makes a motion and the other seconds the motion, a discussion should then follow an alternating pro and con scenario. When the pros and cons start to repeat, vote on the motion and be done with it.

- **Open Meetings.** To eliminate suspicion and rumors, board meetings should be open to all owners for the purpose of auditing (that means to listen but not participate). Allow for an owner forum preceding the meeting to answer questions or allow members to make statements. Once the meeting starts, they should be welcome to stay but not interrupt business. To make that clear, have them sit away from the board meeting table. The value of maintaining open meetings is to eliminate the "us and them" mentality that can crop up when meetings are closed. Few homeowners want to be at odds with their neighbors. It's important not to create an illusion of pecking order. If non-board members are welcome to the meetings, they'll get a taste of what happens and could become potential volunteers.

- **Keep a Sense of Humor.** It's very important to keep business from becoming ponderous or confrontational. There are few topics in HOAs that are life or death. If someone gets overwrought or agitated, it's time to ratchet up the mirthmeter. If a particular member makes a habit of being obnoxious, insist in private that they either leave it at home, not attend the meeting, or step down off the board, as it applies.

Well-run board meetings are an essential tool for a board that wants to get things done rather than respond to emergencies. Boards that know what they want and where they are heading have meetings that take steps toward their goals. Above all, they avoid letting their meetings wander into the morass of gossip and endless debate.

Hosting Annual Meetings

It can be difficult for an HOA to convince residents to make time for the annual meeting. How can you compete with soccer practice, work schedules, and even entertainment? While it's tough, there are several things you can do:

- **Plan Ahead.** Successful promoters do it early and often (promoting, that is). One idea whose time has come is the Management Planning Calendar. Since you budget a year in advance, why not schedule maintenance events and meetings a year in advance? If you do, who could possibly say they are tied up next year?

- **Seduce Your Audience.** Make each owner feel special, as if the show couldn't go on without them, instead of just like another spoke in the wheel. Make the message: We need YOU!

- **Punch Up the Program.** Make the steak "sizzle." Include a drawing for those that show up, like a dinner for two or a gift certificate from an area merchant that everyone uses.

- **Include a Recognition Program.** Include an awards ceremony to honor community volunteers. Give plaques, certificates, and gift certificates. Be creative and make it fun.

- **Eat Well.** Why not have this event catered with a menu too good to pass up? Have their mouth water just reading the menu. Make it a night to remember. If your social fund is sparse, potluck barbecues and holiday themes work well. Dessert only is good, too.

- **Consider Libations.** Depending on the crowd, after-meeting beverages could be in order... enough for socializing but not for an all-nighter.

- **Casino Night.** Organize a casino night using play money and prizes for the big winners.

- **Stay on Schedule.** The annual meeting need not last more than two hours. Plan to keep the action moving so that folks can come and go on time if they want to. If they want to stay because they're having fun...great!

It's just a fact of life that an HOA must compete against numerous other priorities when seeking a share of members' time. Rather than bemoan their disinterest, energize your annual meeting. Make it a night to remember. If you do it well, they'll actually look forward to next year.

Conclusion

If your board has followed our advice and successfully given up the day-to-day management of the HOA, then regular board meetings provide the main means by which the board conducts its business. It is essential to make sure these meetings are handled in an efficient manner. Proper preparation, setting, ground rules, and a clear agenda can go a long way to ensuring that your HOA functions as intended.

Six:
Rules: Carrots or Sticks?

Rule creation and rule enforcement can be the most contentious and difficult aspect of HOA management. Everyone loves HOA rules as long as they restrict someone else's freedom for the sake of property values. It's when they restrict our own freedoms that they suddenly seem capricious and unfair. The value of a rule is often in the eye of the rule maker. However, properly constructed rules protect the property values of the HOA, allow for fair and equal access to amenities, and create a more harmonious community.

Keep It Professional

A better rule-making process starts with the core assumption that members are reasonable adults, not delinquents who need constant monitoring. Too often, boards adopt a defensive position when it comes to rules and rule breakers. We encourage you to avoid such thinking. Rather than trying to punish violators, boards will be much better off if rules are written with incentives for compliance. After all, these are neighbors. Carrots are much better than sticks. With that in mind, here are some basic principles to help guide your rule-making process.

- **Be Consistent.** From the member's point of view, the rules can often feel like they originate in the personal whims of the board, rather than any reasonable standard. This can lead to rebellion and discord among the members, particularly when the rules deal with the four "P"s: People, Property, Parking, and Pets. Living in close proximity is the norm in HOAs, and as such, requires some personal sacrifice. Sacrifice is always more palatable when it serves the common good, rather than the personal whims of the board. For example, when creating architectural rules, it is advisable to consult with architects and real estate agents. Let these outside "experts" help you create architectural rules that truly serve the goal of high property values and not the personal tastes of the board.

- **Put All Rules in Writing.** It's surprising how many HOAs have unwritten rules that an offender doesn't discover until they break them. Judges, however, don't like the idea of unwritten rules and often punish HOAs that have them. All rules should be written in plain English.

- **Always Circulate Proposed Rules for Thirty Days.** The most important step in getting community buy-in for new rules is to allow comment before the board approves them. HOA boards can get myopic about the need for rules. Problems that loom large to a board may be of little importance to the majority of members. The board can make much ado about nothing. Worse, the board can fan the flames of rebellion by enacting an unpopular rule. (Is that tar I smell?) There is no rule so urgent that it couldn't wait for a thirty-day member review and comment. Proposed rules circulated to the members generally gain greater buy-in and compliance, rather than defiance.

- **Keep Rules to a Minimum.** Rules breed like rabbits. According to the *Atlanta Journal*, "The Ten Commandments contain 297 words. The Bill of Rights is stated in 463 words. Lincoln's Gettysburg Address contains 266 words. A recent federal directive to regulate the price of cabbage contains 26,911 words." HOAs run more harmoniously when they seek to keep their rules to the bare minimum necessary for their mandate. A board shouldn't become like Congress, which seems to create laws just to justify its existence.

- **Don't Duplicate Local Laws.** The board should not involve itself in rule-making that is normally handled by professional law enforcement. The police are far better equipped to handle drug dealers, out-of-control parties, and domestic disputes. All such complaints should be referred to law enforcement by the parties most directly offended, the neighbors.

- **Never Write a Rule to Control One Individual.** In HOAs rules often proliferate when boards overreact to challenges from homeowners. Rather than taking the time to understand a particular point of view, the Board promulgates a rule intended to smite the scofflaw. It's an age-old struggle... individuals testing legal loopholes and governments trying to plug them. Like grains of sand on the beach, there are an infinite number of loopholes and loophole plugs. There are better ways to deal with scofflaws. Start by listening. Then seek common ground, and remember compromise isn't a dirty word. It's often much cheaper than the cost of a lawsuit.

- **Discontinue Rules That Have Outlived Their Usefulness.** Another way to avoid rule proliferation is to make sure that HOAs remove rules that may have seemed vitally important years ago but no longer have value. If it's no longer worth enforcing, remove it from your books.

- **Make All Rules Available for Inspection.** In the age of the Internet every HOA should have its rules available 24/7 on a website. This helps members and prospective buyers alike. A buyer with an RV might be a little bit upset to learn of a no-RV rule after closing. Having your rules available at all times makes them clear to all concerned.

- **Enforce Rules Equally.** When it comes to HOA rule enforcement, it can sometimes seem that it's "who you know" that determines who gets enforced upon and who doesn't. If a rule is worthy, it should be enforced on everyone, including board members and their friends. This way, the board doesn't have to fight the arguments that so-and-so violated the same rule and nothing happened or that the board is immune from prosecution.

- **The Board Is Not the Enforcer.** Any board that wants to be goal-focused and oversight-driven should do its best to stay away from playing the enforcer. There does need to be some regular way of assessing whether or not problem rules— parking rules for example—are followed. However, in most instances, rule enforcement should begin with a neighbor's complaint. We recommend that such regular enforcement be left to the hired manager. After all, you are neighbors with the offender. There's nothing that can sour the relationships in a community like neighbors fining neighbors.

•   **Start With Gentle Reminders Rather Than Punitive Measures.** Some rules are perennial problems. New members move in and older members forget. The member newsletter provides a great forum for gentle reminders about these rules. Reminders are often the best way to gain compliance and keep harmony. Fines and other punitive measures should be a last resort.

•   **Require Complaints in Writing.** It's too easy to make a phone call at all hours of the night. Require the details of the complaint to be put in writing or don't accept the complaint.

•   **Complainer Should Be the First to Ask for Compliance from the Offender.** Before a complaint is accepted by the board, the HOA rules should require the complainer to speak with the offender and ask for a correction before handing the matter over to the board.

•   **Provide a Right of Appeal.** It's as American as apple pie to have an excuse, and extenuating circumstances may actually be legitimate. Appeals are not only fair, but expected. The board should never engage in a game of "gotcha." Look for ways to catch someone doing good.

Conclusion

At the end of the day, rules and enforcement are an important if unpleasant part of the duties of an HOA board. Too often they become contentious, with the board (over)reacting to a perceived slight by a single member or a small band of rebels. Remember, the rules exist for the harmonious functioning of the HOA. If the rules and the process by which you create them destroys your community spirit, the board has already lost before it has even started.

Seven:
Recruitment Made Easy

It's an all-too-common occurrence in an HOA. The same few people volunteer regularly while the majority appear apathetic and disinterested. Too often, the call goes out, and no one answers. Hello? Is anybody out there? For those doing more than their fair share of the work, it's all too easy to fall back into a defensive posture. Subtle resentments can grow. "I guess no one cares."

In our experience, many of them do care. It's not that no one wants to volunteer. It's just that the reasons they are given for doing so are often, well, too uninspiring. While "serving the community" and "protecting your interests" may seem motivation enough, where's the excitement? Where's the glory in it all? Perhaps it's the job description that needs a makeover, not the membership?

Throughout this book we have encouraged you to re-envision the job of board member and volunteer. In this section, we want to help you think through how this new vision for your board can help you recruit not only capable board members but quality volunteers as well.

You Already Know What to Do

Many good candidates fail to step forward because the job is not explained to them properly. There is a natural fear of the unknown, fear of being trapped in an open-ended commitment. A huge part of wooing volunteers is defining it in terms that make it clear it's something to look forward to, not endless drudgery, or worse. Painting a vision for the job is everything.

You may not realize it but you already know what to do. A huge part of recruiting and maintaining volunteers is making sure your board acts efficiently to get things done. Getting things done has everything to do with how you run your meetings. Well-run meetings, with action agendas, time limits, and fair rules that are followed regularly, go a long way to attracting high-quality people. Think about it this way. Quality volunteers want to know their time will be well spent. A well-run meeting goes a long way to demonstrating that their service to the community won't be time wasted.

Director Solicitation Letter

When recruiting new board members becomes a necessity, the board has an opportunity to properly outline the scope of the job and the expected time commitment. Here is a sample solicitation letter that outlines director duties:

To All Members of Nottacare Condominium,
At the annual meeting to be held April first, two positions for director of the board will be voted on. Anyone that is an owner in good standing of Nottacare (current in HOA payments and no outstanding violations) is eligible to run in this election.

Overview of Director Duties:
The board has the authority to direct Nottacare business, including maintenance and financial oversight, rules enforcement, and architectural design approval. The board has the authority to hire and oversee the professional management company.
The board meets four times a year for two hours to review Nottacare business and to make decisions and enact policy. Between those meetings, there may be an occasional special meeting to deal with an urgent matter that can't wait for a regularly scheduled board meeting. The president has the authority to act on behalf of the board between meetings, as long as the matter is authorized by the governing documents or in line with the approved budget.

Serving on the board gives you direct impact and influence on how Nottacare business is handled. While a management, financial, or construction background is helpful, no special training is required, other than the willingness and availability to serve. The office of director carries a term of three years each.

All Nottacare members have a responsibility to serve in some capacity. We hope you will consider running for the board. If you are interested in running, you may be nominated by another owner or by yourself. If you are interested in being nominated, please email that desire and your contact information to info@nottacare.org or mail to Nottacare Condominum, 123 Easy St, Anytown USA by no later than March 25th. Please contact me if you have any questions.

I.M Daboss daboss@nottacare.org
President - Nottacare Condominum
Phone 555.555.5555

Increasing Participation

A common HOA board question is "How do we get better participation from our members with board and committee work?" On the one hand, one of the reasons people buy into HOAs is to reduce personal responsibility, such as for exterior maintenance. On the other hand, there are many willing and talented members that could and would participate if given the right set of circumstances. There is an art to recruiting volunteers. Posting a notice is not the right approach. You must woo them on many levels and over time. Here are a couple of proven methods:

- **Communicate Regularly.** A frequent complaint of members is not being kept informed. If you are to draw out volunteers, it's critical that they know there is an ongoing need. Also, some members develop a suspicious nature about board motives when kept in the dark and use it as an excuse not to be involved. Let them know what you're up to, early and often! Repeated pleas for help will have their effect. A newsletter and flyer distribution box (the kind used by real estate agents) is an inexpensive and convenient way to get the word out.

- **Give Credit Where Credit Is Due.** People love recognition. Make sure that directors, committee members, and other volunteers are given formal recognition for their efforts by way of meetings, minutes, and newsletters. Use every opportunity where there is an audience. Be specific in your praise. For example, point out members that show superior landscaping abilities. (They are obvious candidates for the Landscape Committee.) Award Certificates of Achievement at the annual meeting. Remember to recognize faithful volunteers doing more mundane day-to-day tasks like light bulb replacement or trash pick-up. It is a wise board that makes a point of recognizing mere effort for its own merits.

- **Socialize the Membership.** People tend to want to help those that they know personally. However, many are shy and don't make friends easily. The HOA can promote several social events annually to facilitate the process. Consider a spring cleanup party, pool party, or potluck. It will help create community and break down barriers.

- **Assign Real Jobs to Do.** It's been said, "A committee takes minutes and wastes hours." There is nothing more frustrating than a job with no job description or substance. There is real work to do at each HOA. Directors and committee members should have clear "marching orders" detailing exactly what the objectives are, the time frame, and the money available to help get the task done.

- **Be an Encourager.** It is incumbent on the board to take the lead in cultivating volunteers. The successful leader motivates by persuasion and not authority. Remember, "A servant does not lower himself but elevates others."

- **Try the Ask.** This is a little-used technique. Many folks don't think they're needed or talented enough. A personal request can go a long way in getting these folks to step up. Something as simple as "You know, you would be really good at (fill in the blank)." You will be surprised how many will respond with "yes."

- **Respect Their Time.** Part of what keeps volunteers away is fear of over-commitment. The board should be very sensitive to time demands on volunteers. Board meetings should be few and goal-focused. When wooing volunteers, make sure to explain the time requirements for the job. The properly managed HOA should demand hours, not days or weeks of volunteer time each year.

- **Demystify the Job.** While having special training or talent can be a bonus to a board or committee position, it isn't required. Encourage those that simply want to serve because they have the time and interest.

- **Aim High.** Look for ways to pique the interest of high achievers. If you aim too low, folks don't think you need them. Identify several projects that take real thought, planning and work but demonstrate visible results. Assign those special projects to members that like to "gitter done."

- **Carry Out 365-Day Recruiting.** The month prior to the annual meeting is not the only time to look for board candidates and volunteers. New members often have an interest in getting plugged in and are ripe for the picking at move-in. Whenever a special project or event materializes, look outside the board for someone to do it.

- **Don't Forget the One-Trick Pony.** Provide options for "one-project" volunteers. Some folks like the idea of a short-term commitment to get one thing done. Projects like these are often the training ground for long-term volunteers.

Getting the ball rolling to increase participation is one of the most rewarding efforts a board can achieve. In a motivated HOA, a synergy develops with a result that far exceeds the sum of the parts.

Conclusion

Having a proper goal-driven, can-do attitude for your board goes a long way to helping recruit the volunteers your HOA needs to thrive. The rest of it is all about how you ask. A board that is reactive, constantly responding to the latest problem, will find it difficult to recruit volunteers. After all, very few people want a stronger sense of crisis in their lives.

Eight:
Rentals: Manage the Owner, Not the Tenant

Absentee owners and tenants provide the stuff of nightmares for HOAs. There is nothing more frustrating than a misbehaving tenant who cannot be punished directly by the HOA. Fortunately, there are a few things a board can do to avoid this disaster.

The Rental Policy

A strong defense against unruly renters starts with the HOA's rental policy. Make sure your governing documents have one. Without one, the owners have the right to rent out their property to whomever they please, whenever they please. If an HOA board finds that it does not have a policy on rentals, it will need to amend its governing documents to add one.

There is a good reason for many HOAs to restrict the number of rentals allowed. For one thing, when the number of rentals exceeds about one-third of the total, some lenders restrict lending because the character of the property changes from owner-occupied to investment property. Investment property loans are higher risk, and investors are historically less willing to invest money in maintenance and repairs. This jeopardizes a lender's collateral and increases the odds of loan default. Federal Housing Administration (FHA) loans for condominiums now have a 49% rental restriction level.

Besides restricting the number of rentals allowed, many HOAs also find it beneficial to create a minimum rental period. This is usually intended to prevent short-term rentals, except in vacation-oriented HOAs. This restriction is becoming all the more important as Internet rental services become more popular.

Make sure your governing documents allow the board to create reasonable rules and regulations regarding rentals.

One thing should be made clear—the HOA has no authority either to enforce rules or to levy fines directly on tenants. This is the responsibility of the landlord owner. But levying fines against non-resident owners for violations by their tenants doesn't quickly remedy a problem. For this reason, the board should add the following provisions to its rental policy:

1. A breach by the tenant of the governing documents or rules is a breach of the owner's rental agreement. [This requirement would allow the owner to evict a tenant if appropriate.]

2. Owners are required to take corrective action against a tenant, up to and including eviction, in case of a violation.

3. Owners are required to provide their tenants the homeowner association governing documents and rules as a condition of renting. The statement "Tenant has received copies of, read, and understood, and will comply with the HOA's rules and regulations" must be included in the rental agreement.

Finally, since restricting or prohibiting rentals affects an owner's fundamental property rights, a Rental Restriction Policy should be enacted only as an amendment to the governing documents. The board should not do this on its own. Such a proposed policy should be reviewed by an attorney specializing in homeowner association law.

Tenants from Heaven

Once the board has a proper rental policy in place, much of the heavy lifting necessary to avoid problems with "tenants from hell" has been completed. Generally speaking, both the landlord and the tenant want the highest and best returns on their investments. What benefits the HOA will also benefit them.

Besides having a proper rental policy, the board can take some steps to assure a more successful tenancy. For one, the board should make clear to both the tenant and the landlord that they are expected to comply with all HOA rules. Of course, the tenant has to know the rules in order to comply. It's up to the landlord to comply and failure can be a violation fineable against the landlord. Include renters with other residents who receive information about the rules.

The landlord should provide the board with:

1. Name and contact information for the tenant.

2. Vehicle information (make, model, plate number for each).

3. Copy of the rental agreement that references the HOA rules as a condition of the agreement. (This is very important because it places the burden on the landlord to advise the tenant of rules and shows that the tenant received that information.)

While the HOA cannot require it, common sense and good management practice indicate that landlords should also:

1. Perform credit checks on prospective tenants.

2. Check several previous landlord references (HINT: The most recent landlord may have a vested interest in getting this tenant out.)

3. Have read and understand the state's landlord-tenant laws.

4. Identify all occupants in the lease by name to avoid "musical" tenants.

While the landlord is the key to properly framing a tenant's role within the HOA, it's also important that the board, manager, and owners refrain from treating tenants like second-class citizens. When treated with respect and like owner-members of the community, they usually act the part, by taking care of the property and respecting the neighbors. Treat renters like owners and reap tenants from heaven.

Conclusion

As in all things related to HOAs, when it comes to rentals victory goes to the proactive. A board that wants to lead its HOA rather than be led by it should examine its governing documents to make sure it has an appropriate rental policy and then should enforce it. Making sure that the tenant and landlord have a clear understanding of their responsibilities before the tenant occupies the property goes a long way to creating a harmonious relationship between tenants and the HOA.

Nine:
Proactive Maintenance, Not
Crisis Management

While all HOAs age, not all of them age gracefully. Dry rot, extensive wood-boring insect damage, leaking roofs, and hefty special assessments seem to be the order of the day. Letting maintenance slide year after year is not the answer. Owners' property in HOAs that are well-maintained will sell faster and for more money. It is a matter of protecting and maintaining the asset, a board's primary and legal responsibility.

Keys to the Maintenance Journey

So how can those HOAs that want to maintain their assets do so with a minimal amount of funds and energy? There are several "keys" which may assist in the maintenance journey:

- **Get Committed.** The board first needs to go on record that it is committed philosophically to preventive maintenance. Consider enacting a formal written resolution approved by the board that mandates professional quality maintenance of the property as a foundation of this commitment. As boards change, they will be held to this standard.

- **Get Organized.** Find volunteers for a maintenance committee. If any of your members have experience in construction, design, or architecture, so much the better. Next, put together a job description for the committee outlining the major responsibilities and timelines for completion of certain tasks.

- **Develop a Component List.** Besides the obvious like roofs, paint, paving, etc., there may be other not-so-obvious components. Review your documents to identify all the components that your HOA is obligated to maintain. If there is confusion regarding maintenance responsibility for "limited" common areas like a unit's deck, you may wish to consult your attorney. If your community is older, you may want to do this anyway to make sure the documents conform to current laws. Amending them will clarify maintenance responsibilities that are vague or absent.

- **Clarify Your Responsibilities.** Your insurance agent needs to know which components the HOA will be taking responsibility for and how that might affect coverage and premiums. (Insurance coverage disputes between HOA and homeowners are common because of poorly written documents and failure by the board to properly define responsibility.) The key is to bring clarity and distinction to those components that will be maintained by the HOA, as opposed to those maintained by the homeowners themselves.

- **Physically Inspect the Components.** Many boards have never taken the time to walk around the property on a "maintenance inspection," and those that do often do not possess the proper skills. Choose the people carefully that will perform this duty. In addition, include reputable, licensed, and qualified contractors, engineering or architectural consultants, or certified building inspectors. These people have a trained eye that will pick up potential problems that laymen would miss. Although they may charge for their time, they will save money in the long run.

- Once you have completed your walk-through, categorize all components in the following manner:

  - Building Components: Roofs, gutters, windows, siding and trim, decks, garage doors, heating/AC units, elevators, etc.

  - Site Components: Pavement, concrete, area lighting, fences, entry monuments, etc.

- Landscaping Components: Time clocks, sprinkler heads, controllers, water features, etc.

- Recreational Components: Pool, spa, sauna, tennis courts, playground, exercise room, clubhouse, etc.

- **Develop a Maintenance Plan.** Define the guideline for maintenance of each component assuring professionally done lasting repairs. Avoid the "band-aid" mentality... it will cost you dearly. Use your service providers to determine reasonable methods and costs.

- **Allocate the Funds.** The best maintenance plan in the world is useless if not properly funded. Since money comes from the operating budget and increasing the maintenance budget is not popular, it is critical to have the plan that justifies the budget. Build the budget around the maintenance program, not vice versa.

- **Follow Up on the Work.** Have the maintenance committee or property manager do monthly (or at least quarterly) inspections and put the observations in writing for the file. The report can be used as a checklist for the maintenance or landscaping people doing corrective work.

- **Build Service Continuity.** Establish long-term relationships with reputable service providers for continuity. Once a provider understands and provides the service you are looking for, why reinvent the wheel every time the board changes? Check each vendor's costs at budget time to confirm that the HOA is getting a competitive price.

If a preventive maintenance program is implemented, the HOA can not only help protect itself from unscheduled special assessments, but will enhance the unit values as well. The purpose of preventive maintenance is to spend some money now to save a lot later. It is a legacy deeply appreciated by those that follow.

Managing Large Projects

Winter is the time of year that the board should be arranging and reviewing proposals for fair-weather renovation projects. Painting, siding, fencing, pool replastering, and roofing are but a few of the major items that fit the profile. There are several practical reasons for starting the process early:

- **Contractors Are More Available.** Winter is a slow time for many contractors. This means they have the time to consider your work and produce a good proposal.

- **Better Pricing.** When work is slow, many contractors are willing to offer better pricing to "seal the deal." Sometimes the work you want done can be performed during the winter months. If you agree to start the project now, you just may save a significant amount of money.

- **Preferential Scheduling.** If you accept a contractor's proposal now, you can often get preferred scheduling. Set the date early. If you wait, you may not make the schedule at all.

Starting in the winter gives the board plenty of time to accomplish the following:

- **Arrange for Funds.** If you haven't accumulated enough reserve funds, you will need several months to discuss, approve, and collect a special assessment.

- **Coordinate with Residents.** If the project is extensive and disruptive, you will want to warn residents well in advance. This will give them the opportunity to work around the project or even plan vacations strategically.

- **Verify License, Bonding, and Insurance.** Most states require building contractors to be licensed and to show their state license number on proposals, websites, and business cards. Where licensing is required, a bond is often required, as well as certain kinds of insurance, such as liability and workers compensation, if the contractor has employees. Insist on evidence of this.

- **Get References.** Only use contractors that have a good track record in your community. Make sure the references are for work that is comparable in size and complexity to yours. It is not uncommon for small contractors to get in over their heads. Require evidence that they have performed similar work for other HOAs.

- **Get Named as Additional Insured.** Insist on getting a current copy of the contractor's liability insurance coverage directly from the insurance agent. If you accept the proposal, require that the HOA be included on this insurance as an "additional insured," and get an appropriate and current insurance certificate from the contractor's insurance agent to prove it.

- **Make Progress Payments.** Do not make advance payments on the project work unless there are custom materials involved. If there are custom materials, pay the material provider directly and have them delivered directly to the site. A contractor's insistence on upfront payment is often a red flag that the contractor may be using your money to pay for some other job's labor or supply bills. You could be left high and dry with uncompleted work. Instead, use progress payments that pay for work actually completed. Be sure to inspect the work to verify completion.

- **Consider Paying for a Performance Bond.** For large and expensive projects, requiring a performance bond provides assurance that the contractor will perform or another contractor can be hired to finish the job. It costs extra but is often worth it.

- **Get Lien Waivers.** When making payments, have the contractor provide a lien waiver for the amount tendered. A lien waiver is the contractor's promise that he has paid for all labor, material, and supply bills related to the work to date. Keep in mind that if your contractor "forgets" to pay his suppliers, or subcontractors and material suppliers, those folks have the right to place a mechanic's lien on the property to secure their debt. It's a good policy to require that copies of all paid supply, material, and labor bills be attached to and referenced in the signed lien waiver.

For substantial projects, it's important to involve an attorney who can draft or review the contract. There's a lot riding on what the board is obligating the HOA to. There is much planning involved in rolling out a successful renovation project. Forget the leap of faith on this one. The safety net just may not be there when you land. Get a jump on your renovation projects and get a quality job done on schedule and at the best price.

Creating a Maintenance Calendar

One way for a board to move from a reactive stance to a proactive stance when it comes to maintenance is to create a multi-year calendar (on-line calendar programs are excellent at this) or more simply, at least a list of last service dates for HOA components and due dates for the next service. For instance, if the board has a list that says the pool was resurfaced four years ago with an expected life of six years, the board can plan for that expense in its budgeting process. A high-quality reserve study done by a certified professional should help the board greatly in thinking about adding long-term replacement projects to this maintenance list, such as roof and siding replacement. However, there are other maintenance tasks that should be scheduled on a much more frequent basis. Here is a list of common components in an HOA that need to be checked often.

- **Painting** is one of the largest elements of routine common area maintenance for many HOAs. Poorly maintained paint will fail prematurely. Touch-up should be done annually. Wood trim should be painted every three to four years. The complete painting of buildings should be done every six to eight years.

- **Drainage.** Rain and sprinkler run-off can create problems for the lawn, landscaping, and underground building areas. The landscape contractor can often provide for drainage corrections that will mitigate these areas.

- **Salt Air Corrosion.** Salt air found at coastal locations can rapidly deteriorate and short-circuit light fixtures, elevator electronics, fire sprinkler system plumbing, electrical boxes, and door hardware. These should be checked every year.

- **Concrete Sidewalks and Driveways.** Concrete needs to be inspected annually for cracks and raised areas, as well as degradation of the surface. Raised areas create a trip hazard, which can be corrected by grinding or removal and replacement.

- **Asphalt Paving.** Asphalt needs to be repaired and seal-coated every three to five years to properly protect it so it will achieve its maximum useful life of twenty-five to thirty years.

- **Roofs.** Roofs need to be part of a spring and fall maintenance plan. They need to be inspected, repaired, and cleaned by a qualified roofing maintenance contractor.

- **Roof Gutters and Downspouts.** These should be cleaned at least twice a year, more often in "hotspots" where leaf debris is prevalent. Failure to do this causes backups and overflow that damages paint, siding, and landscaping.

- **Playground Equipment.** Playground equipment should be inspected and maintained to ensure child safety.

- **Directional Signage.** Signage should be in good repair and easily readable in order to assist emergency response services like police, fire, and pizza delivery (joke). Directories with names and addresses also facilitate emergency response. The directory should be regularly updated for accuracy.

Deferred maintenance is a sucker bet which will always come back to bite. Using a calendar or other system to regularly replace and maintain common components will help the board create a steady, reasonable operating budget on a year-in and year-out basis.

Proper maintenance is the most important thing a board can do to avoid the dreaded special assessment.

Conclusion

Creating a maintenance calendar and using it is one of the most important steps a board can use to move away from a reactive management style and toward a more proactive management system. The board has a legal and ethical duty to maintain the property values of the HOA. Of course, keeping fees reasonable is an important consideration for any board. The problem arises when the board or the membership refuse to pay the fees necessary for proper maintenance of the property.

Ten:
Insurance

Insurance claims are a frequent area of dispute. All too often, conflict arises because one party is underinsured and hoping another's insurance will pay for a loss. Misunderstandings abound regarding the responsibilities of the HOA and the owners. Governing documents are often vague.

There is a frequent misconception that the HOA will cover all major losses to owner property. To complicate matters, many insurance agents never read the HOA's governing documents and don't understand which coverages are appropriate for their owner clients.

In this section, we will show you how the board, homeowners, and agents can make sense out of this insurance mire. Clarity when it comes to responsibility regarding insurance can save your HOA thousands in deductibles and higher premiums.

Maintenance and Insurance Areas of Responsibility

A policy document called Maintenance and Insurance Areas of Responsibility can eliminate gray areas or gaps in both maintenance and insurance. By identifying building and grounds components and assigning responsibility to either the HOA or the owner, gaps are effectively closed. The idea is to clearly define the point where HOA responsibility stops and owner responsibility begins. If you maintain it, you insure it. For example, repairs to all common water supply and drain lines are an HOA responsibility, but repairs to all unit water supply and drain lines from the connection point with common lines are an owner responsibility. Barring conflicting insurance requirements in the governing documents or state statute, here are reasonable guidelines for the HOA to follow in developing a policy for handling insurance claims:

1. The HOA is responsible for repairing only those things for which it has maintenance responsibility.

2. If the HOA is negligent in maintenance and it results in unit damage, like failing to repair a leaking roof in a timely manner when notified, the HOA is responsible for the damage repairs to the units.

3. Each unit owner is responsible for insuring his own unit and personal property. For example, if a washer hose breaks in Unit A on the 3rd floor, damaging 3A and its two downstairs neighbors, each unit owner would be responsible for insuring the damage suffered within their unit. The HOA's insurance would not be involved.

4. If HOA common area property is damaged by an event that originates within a unit—similar to the event described above—the HOA may hold the unit owner liable for the damage and seek recovery under the liability portion of the unit owner's insurance. This is based on the principle that the HOA has the authority to define who is responsible for repairing common area damage according to the source of the damage. If the damage originates from an HOA-maintained source, the HOA is responsible. If it originates from an owner-maintained source, the owner is responsible. Owners do not have the same policy-making authority as the HOA and can only make claim against a neighbor's policy if negligence can be proven.

Once the Areas of Responsibility are completed, approved, and distributed to the owners and their insurance carriers, all have the same point of reference. Bottom line: Maintenance requests and insurance claims are expedited and the HOA is only paying for things that are its responsibility. One caveat: For every rule, there is an exception. As exceptions are identified, the Areas of Responsibility should be revised.

The importance of the Maintenance and Insurance Areas of Responsibility document becomes all the more clear when you understand the broad "blanket" coverage offered by most HOA policies. In effect, the insurance carrier looks to the HOA to determine whether it should pay a claim or not. If given no direction, the carrier usually errs on the side of the homeowner.

Self-Insurance

Another cost-cutting technique is to raise the deductible to $2500 or higher and have the HOA pay for smaller claims (also called self-insurance). Raising the deductible will often result in a dollar-for-dollar savings in premiums. Premium savings can be assigned to a budget category called "Insurance Deductible" to cover insurance losses that fall under the deductible.

However, reducing premiums cannot be an excuse for underinsuring your HOA. It is important that the board makes sure items like Directors and Officers policies are carried to protect the finances of the HOA when a claim must be made.

Limit Your Liability

Volunteers serve on an HOA Board for a variety of reasons. Retirees may have time to give to the community, others serve to protect their assets, while others serve to fill a void. Regardless of the reason they serve, volunteer board members have liability exposure for actions taken or not taken. Board members are responsible for HOA finances, policy-making, and signing contracts. As we outlined earlier in the book, these responsibilities involve the fiduciary duties of care, loyalty, and honesty, which are elements of the "Business Judgment Rule."

Here are some dos and don'ts to keep you out of trouble:

• **Never Use HOA Funds for Personal Reasons, Even as a Loan.** Many embezzlers started out as "borrowers."

• **Never Misrepresent Your Authority**. In situations such as negotiating with a contractor, never make decisions or sign contracts when that authority belongs to the board as a whole or the board president.

• **Stay Informed About HOA Business.** Read all HOA related correspondence and minutes.

- **Use Consultants When Expertise Is Called For.** Guessing at complex solutions only creates complex problems.

- **Attend All Board Meetings.** If unable to attend, make sure the meeting minutes reflect the reason for absence.

- **Voice Dissenting Opinions to Board Votes When Appropriate.** And make sure the dissent is recorded in the meeting minutes.

- **Be Familiar with the Governing Documents.** When in doubt, consult with a knowledgeable attorney.

If you inadvertently stumble, a suit may be filed against the board and you personally, as a member of a board. All is not lost! Bylaws typically provide that the HOA will indemnify (protect and defend) board members if the conduct meets certain standards like those reflected in the Business Judgment Rule.

The HOA should have a Directors and Officers Liability insurance policy that provides for legal defense. This is extremely important, and not all Directors and Officers policies provide for this contingency. If your board is not covered, contact the HOA insurance carrier as soon as possible.

Liability exposure should not be taken lightly. Prevent overexposure by understanding the obligations, limitations, and scope of authority. Add a little common sense and proper liability insurance, and you're covered!

Conclusion

The HOA must be careful about how many insurance claims it turns in. Frequency of claims affects the HOA's premium level and insurability. HOAs that file too many claims get their coverage canceled. Assigning certain insurance responsibilities to the owners reduces the HOA's exposure and keeps insurance affordable. It's the board's responsibility to turn the vagaries of the governing documents into a practical policy. Creating a Maintenance and Insurance Areas of Responsibility policy is prudent for every HOA board. The work that goes into developing this policy will reward the HOA by reducing conflicts and promoting harmony.

Eleven:
Keeping Your Organization
Financially Healthy

Could you imagine a board of directors for a corporation that didn't know its way around a financial report? Yet this is an all-too-prevalent reality in the world of HOAs. In this area, like many other areas, the big difference between HOA boards and corporate boards is the extent of their experience in managing a large organization.

Perhaps seventy percent of an HOA board's time is spent on the HOA's finances. The board is charged with managing the fees collected by the HOA for the benefit of the members. Including the members' homes and common amenities, it isn't uncommon for an HOA's assets to exceed a million dollars in value, with annual budgets in the tens of thousands or more.

Despite this, a surprising number of HOAs manage their own books, without using standardized accounting practices. Boards who manage their own finances often stumble, collecting too little to meet their needs. They have trouble keeping up on maintenance and can find themselves forced to use expensive special assessments to pay for repairs, which could easily have been paid for if they had saved adequate reserves. They often use a cash-based accounting system, in a program like Quickbooks. This works fairly well for budgeting purposes. It is easy to track expenses and see exactly how they compare to the budget, but it becomes a real problem when trying to track delinquencies or manage debts, and when planning for maintenance needs years down the road.

More than this, it is an unfortunate truth that most embezzlement happens to small HOAs that manage their own affairs. While it is the big embezzlement by a management company that makes the news, it is rare and easy to avoid if you know what to do. (We'll talk more about this later.) However, the vast majority of embezzlement happens when a treasurer is given sole control over the finances and custody of the bank accounts, without any effective oversight. Boards would do well to get a professional management company that uses standard accounting practices and learn to read their financial reports well enough to exercise oversight. A board that uses standard accounting practices and takes a few simple steps can stop most embezzlement before it starts.

All board members ought to be familiar with the basics of an HOA balance sheet and an income and expense statement. Knowing how to use these two reports will allow a board to have the confidence it needs to make long-range plans. It's hard to resurface the pool or purchase picnic tables when you don't know if you have enough money. The balance sheet and the income statement are the key reports that allow a board to plan.

In this chapter, we will not walk you through everything you need to know about financial reports. As we said at the beginning of the book, we aren't here to make you experts. In fact, a huge problem for boards comes in understanding the language of a financial report. We aren't going to teach you all of the terms used on these documents. Instead, we want to use plain English to highlight a few areas where things get confusing.

If you are having trouble understanding your financial reports, we recommend that the treasurer and at least one other board member take a couple of hours and get themselves educated. There are a wide variety of tutorials on the Internet that teach business owners how to read financial statements. (To start, you could read this page on the Securities and Exchange Commission website designed for investors: http://1.usa.gov/1nNASIO, or there is this video: http://bit.ly/1CSqKWQ.) Just remember there are some key differences that we will cover between a financial report for a corporation and that of an HOA.

You could take your financial documents to a CPA who specializes in HOAs and let them help you understand them. (Make sure that the CPA specializes in HOAs, as many CPAs will not be familiar with the particular quirks of an HOA financial statement.)

Instead of teaching you financial basics, we want to focus on how a board can put all these reports together to detect most embezzlement, hold management companies accountable for their spending, and take on projects with confidence. To begin, we need to make sure that you are getting all the information you need from your manager to accomplish these tasks.

Cash or Accrual?

Earlier in this book, we mentioned the need for HOA boards to adopt an accrual-based form of bookkeeping instead of using a cash-based bookkeeping system. Most states require this type of bookkeeping for HOAs of a certain size, and many management companies provide this type of bookkeeping. However, we do find some smaller HOAs, particularly those who try to do their own bookkeeping, still using a cash-based bookkeeping system. There are a few management firms who use cash-based systems as well.

In one sense, a cash-based accounting system seems more intuitive. Income and expenses are added to the books when the money enters or leaves the account. In an accrual-based accounting system, expenses are added to the ledger when incurred, not when paid, and income is added to the ledger when earned, not when it is received.

A cash-based accounting system is much better for making sure you have the cash on hand to make needed purchases. However, HOA boards should not make sudden unplanned purchases. If managed properly, they don't often run into cash-flow crises. If unplanned purchases happen, such purchases usually are for emergency repairs and come from the reserve fund. Cash flow shouldn't be the chief concern of an HOA.

An accrual-based system of accounting does a much better job of giving the board a true picture of the HOA's financial health in the following areas:

- **Depreciation.** An HOA may have purchased a television for the common room years ago at a price of five thousand dollars. In most cash-based accounting systems, that television will still show up on the books as worth five thousand dollars today. However, an accrual system will account for the depreciation (loss of value). On an accrual balance sheet, it may only be worth one hundred dollars.

- **Planning for the Future.** An accrual-based system is much better at showing upcoming income and expenses. For instance, a cash-based system does not account for those bills that have yet to be paid. Suppose an HOA has a large number of outstanding bills from a remodel project. If those bills have not been paid, on a cash balance sheet the HOA will show that it still has much more money than it does. An accrual-based balance sheet will do a much better job of showing exactly what funds it will have left when those bills are paid. This can help the board make decisions about how much it wants to spend on furnishing and decorations for the newly re-carpeted hallways.

- **Delinquencies.** An accrual-based accounting system keeps track of delinquent assessments. A cash-based system does not. Bad debts don't show up on a cash-based accounting system. An accrual-based system allows boards to better track the percentage of these delinquent payments they eventually recover and what percentage is permanently lost. It also allows them to analyze whether or not their HOA has an effective strategy for collecting on late assessments.

Understanding the Balance Sheet

While we said up front that we don't intend to give you a complete primer on how to read financial statements, there is one quirk on HOA balance sheets that is important to mention. They can feel a little tricky until you get the hang of them. The balance sheet is designed to show the financial health of an organization at a given point in time. It shows the assets the HOA owns and controls (including cash) and the debts it owes.

If you are used to reading for-profit balance sheets, HOA finances don't make sense at first glance. The confusion starts to clear when one understands the unique relationship between the HOA and the members. At the beginning of this book, we suggested that the homeowners can be thought of as the stockholders in a company—the HOA. The board works on their behalf. However, there is at least one major difference between the two situations.

In an HOA, the "stockholders" directly control some of the assets of the corporation—the common property. The owners create an HOA to manage the common property of the association. In most cases it does not have direct authority to dispose of that property, even if it might hold title to the property. Many HOA management companies and even a great number of CPAs do not document this unique relationship in a correct manner when they create a balance sheet for an HOA board.

If a corporation spends money on a new roof for the headquarters building, the money on the balance sheet leaves cash and goes across the balance sheet into the roof, which becomes an asset of the corporation. This shows that the value of the corporation hasn't changed. It simply means the organization has placed some of the value it held in cash into the new roof.

However, this familiar accounting practice would be incorrect for an HOA. Since the HOA only manages the clubhouse for the members and does not have direct control over the sale of that asset, any money it spends on a new roof for the clubhouse is an expense. Proper accounting subtracts the money from cash but does not place the roof on the balance sheet as an asset of the HOA.

So does the HOA itself own anything, or is everything owned by the members? In almost every case, the HOA does own some items. While the members may retain direct control of the common property, in most instances, the HOA will own and control the personal property associated with the common property. For instance, the HOA will own the big-screen TV, the couches, and the refrigerator in the common room, even though the members will own (or control) the common room itself. On a properly formatted balance sheet, this personal property will show up as assets of the HOA.

Here is an easy little tool to help board members remember what their HOA owns and what it manages:

1.   To have ownership, the HOA must hold title to the item.

2.   It must be able to dispose of that item without a vote of the members.

Once you understand this little quirk of ownership, a properly constructed balance sheet for an HOA starts to make sense.

Four Essential Reports

In order to keep a clear understanding of the financial health of an HOA, someone must be responsible to create financial reports for the board on a regular basis, preferably monthly. For boards that hire a manager, the manager will create these reports. Self-managed boards must create them on their own. If those reports are in good order and created properly, we believe it should take an educated board no more than fifteen minutes at a board meeting to assess them.

An important step in reducing the amount of time required for a board to understand its financial situation is making sure it is receiving the right information from the manager. A task-oriented and forward-thinking board will ask that its financial reports be emailed to the board twenty-four hours before the meeting, so that valuable meeting time isn't wasted reading them. The following is a list of the four documents you should get from your manager on a monthly basis:

- **A Balance Sheet.** The balance sheet provides a picture of the financial status of an organization at a point in time. It shows a board what it owns and what it owes. It tells the board if it has the money on hand to meet its current obligations.

- **An Income and Expense Statement with a Budget Comparison.** An Income and Expense statement shows a board how much it earned and what expenses it incurred for a given period of time. Boards should ask their manager to make sure that each month they show both the actual and budgeted expenses, as well as the difference between the two. If your manager wants to go above and beyond, they could also show what you spent during the same time period last year. The income statement is the tool a board can use to make sure their manager is spending their funds appropriately.

- **A Statement of Aging Receivables.** One of the important reasons to hire a professional manager is to put in place a strategic plan to collect debts. This statement shows the board their delinquency rate and how well the HOA is doing at collecting on those debts.

- **Bank Statements with a Reconciliation Report Attached.** Each month the manager should provide the board with a copy of its bank statement and a reconciliation report. This will allow the board to make sure it has accurate information when making decisions. It also is an important means of preventing embezzlement. (As we shall see, it remains important for the board to get its own statements from the bank.)

Preventing Embezzlement

A large percentage of embezzlement can be stopped by using the financial reports we have discussed. We aren't going to cover every type of embezzlement in this section. In fact, we have a later short chapter on proper cash controls, which is another key step in avoiding embezzlement. However, a thief who tries to steal money from the assessments or other income of an HOA will leave a paper trail, and an experienced board that knows a couple of tricks can learn to spot this kind of embezzlement quickly before it gets out of control. Let's look at two specific examples.

Theft by a manager or management company may happen when money that is designated for reserves is deposited into the operating account but never transferred to the reserves. This is often done when a management company runs into hard times in its own financial situation. It can be very tempting for an owner or CFO to simply "borrow" the money, rather than place it in the reserve account where it is out of reach. The management company often does so with every intention of putting it back when its own cash flow gets better. Then one thing or another happens, and the management company or the manager is not able to put the money back. With the advent of laser printers and the Internet, management companies have the ability to hide this theft through altering bank statements or creating them out of whole cloth.

This is one important reason we encourage every board to ask for bank statements and a reconciliation report from its manager each time they present financial reports to the board. If your management company is going to try to steal from you in this way, it should at least have to go through the work of putting together a forged statement.

Stopping this embezzlement is quite simple. Every HOA board should have on-line access to its bank accounts and should print off its own bank statements each month. Its treasurer should then be able to quickly compare the statements from the bank with those presented by the management company. If they don't match for some reason, you have a serious problem.

In Portland, Oregon, a management company stole from over thirty different HOAs using this method to the tune of over two million dollars. The theft happened during a three-year timespan, and no one caught it, until one of the boards went to use some of their reserve funds and found that their reserve account was empty. All of that theft could have been avoided if any of these boards had simply taken the extra precaution of having on-line bank account access.

If you want to steal large sums of money from an HOA, it would be hard to do so by including them in the expenses on the income statement. Usually, an astute board will notice that the amount it pays for electricity has suddenly risen. So rather than hiding the theft in all the expenses, many thieves alter the equity on the balance sheet. The thief simply lowers the equity by the amount they have taken. In this way, the expenses are then left alone, and most boards are none the wiser.

There is, however, an easy way to check whether the equity on the current balance sheet is accurate. Each month the treasurer or some other board member should simply add together the equity from the previous month's balance sheet with the net income for the current month and make sure that number is equal to the equity listed on the current balance sheet. If those numbers do not match, there might have been a mistake, but it may also be a sign of theft. Either way, there is some problem or other which needs to be investigated carefully by the board.

Using your financial reports to prevent embezzlement takes little work and is easy when you know what to do. It's a precaution every board should take as a matter of course, and it demands a level of professionalism from your manager, which they should be happy to meet.

Using the Financial Reports to Get Things Done

Financial reports provide the board of an HOA with a picture of its overall financial health. A well-run board that works with a great manager will spend far less time on its financial reports at each meeting than will a board that tries to go it alone and keeps fees at a lower-than-prudent level.

The financial reports allow a board to check up on the manager's performance. The income statement is a great way to see if there are changes in expenses from year to year. Comparing your budgeted amounts with the amounts spent will let the board make necessary mid-year corrections to either expectations or, if necessary, the budget itself.

Financial reports are also an essential tool for planning. A board that has an accurate understanding of its financial situation will be able to make confident decisions about maintenance, repairs, and improvements. Using proper accounting practices and getting correct financial reports from your manager is essential if you want to be a forward-thinking board that spends its time planning for the future, rather than reacting to the past.

If preventing embezzlement and being a forward-thinking board isn't enough to inspire you to use a professional management company for your bookkeeping, then consider this. Good accounting practices and clear financial reports can save an HOA money when it comes to tax time as well. That will be a topic we cover in a future chapter.

Twelve:
Cash Controls

Cash-control procedures can seem like a nuisance. A board may not understand why the treasurer who records the deposit shouldn't be the one who counts the money collected from the laundry room. Often it sees such procedures as cumbersome. If they do get put in place, they are often forgotten and then dropped without anyone noticing.

In this chapter, we want to help you change that. Cash controls aren't just some accountant's idea of a good time. They have a serious purpose. They exist to protect the organization, and board members in particular, from accusations of theft and, more often, errors. They also make sense when you understand the principles behind them. They are designed to ensure trust.

Sometimes a board treasurer or manager can see such procedures as a lack of faith in their integrity, but this is an upside-down way to look at these things. Of all people, treasurers should want to have these kinds of controls in place, so they can clearly demonstrate to the board that nothing deceitful has happened with the HOA's money. Proper cash control procedures are the best defense against suspicion and false accusations for a board treasurer or manager.

They are also a vital tool a board can use to make sure that its management company is handling its funds in a proper fashion. They are an integral part of a board's responsibility to oversee the management company it has hired to take care of the work. The goal here isn't to find something wrong with the management company. The goal is to create a transparent system that allows the board to trust that its funds are handled properly.

No matter how many times we say it, we can't emphasize enough that well-run boards spend less time focused on crises and more time focused on proactive tasks designed to preserve and improve their HOAs. They get things done. They can do this because they aren't spending time worrying and fretting over the latest misstep. Proper cash controls are just another piece in that puzzle, and the truth is that almost every board can improve its cash controls. For boards that receive significant amounts of cash from amenities or other sources, putting in place some clear procedures and holding both board members and their manager accountable to them can be a great project for the board.

For a board interested in improving, the best way to start is by mapping the current system. How does the money get from the laundry room to the operating account? How does money get from the operating account to the reserve accounts, and what is the system for approving expenditures? Once the board has a good idea of how the cash is handled within the organization, this chapter will help them decide on needed changes.

What Should Happen with Our Money?

Cash-control principles begin with one simple concept. To minimize embezzlement and mistakes, separate individuals should take custody of incoming funds, record those funds in the books, and have authorization to spend the HOA's funds. Keeping these three responsibilities as separate as possible makes it much more difficult for theft or mistakes to damage your HOA.

In most instances, a board's management company will take custody of incoming funds and will record them on the HOA's books. This in and of itself isn't a problem, as long as separate people at the management company handle these tasks. The management company may also be authorized to spend the HOA's money for expenses. Again, this isn't a problem as long as such authority is limited, the board exercises proper oversight, and it retains some control over authorization.

We recognize that the principle above is an ideal that almost no HOA or management company will meet perfectly. What it can do is show the board where it needs to exercise more caution and where to put its oversight efforts. To start, part of proper oversight is understanding the systems your management company has in place for taking custody of and recording your funds.

It is all too common for a small HOA to try to cut costs by using its treasurer as its bookkeeper. We believe that this decision is a bit penny smart and pound foolish. The board should use the treasurer's expertise to provide effective oversight for the management company. If the treasurer does the work, most often no one is effectively overseeing them. This leaves the HOA much more vulnerable to mistakes and embezzlement than if it had hired a management company.

This isn't to say that having a management company will solve all the board's problems. In the last chapter, we told you about thirty HOAs in Portland, Oregon, who lost their reserve funds when the management company presented them with altered bank statements and the CFO stole the money. This theft happened because all three cash-control functions were given to one person at the management company. The CFO took custody of the funds, recorded the funds, and was authorized to spend the funds.

While this situation provided the opportunity for embezzlement, what allowed it to flourish was the lack of oversight by the HOA boards. Previously, we told you that all boards should receive and review their own copies of their bank statements, rather than depend upon those given to them by the management company. We would also now add that the board should expect its management company to keep these three cash control functions separate so that no one person can damage the HOA in this way.

If for some reason your management firm cannot accomplish this, it is the board's responsibility to make sure it retains some of these cash-control functions for itself. For instance, if the manager records the cash received on the books for the HOA, then perhaps the board treasurer should be responsible for opening the drop box or collecting the change from the laundry room. This way, these functions still remain separated.

One quick note before we move forward. We recognize that not every board will hire a manager to help with its bills. However, the processes for a self-managed board will be similar but divided among board members. This allows the board to provide its own internal oversight and avoid embezzlement by one of its own.

Funds Received

When fees are left in a drop box or when the laundry machine is full of quarters, someone must take possession of that money for the organization. It must be recorded on the books of the HOA, and it must then be deposited in the bank. In each one of the steps, there are best practices that can be followed to provide a clear trail for the money and minimize the risk of something unfortunate taking place. The goal of these practices is to keep any one person from having sole responsibility for the funds.

- **Collect Fees Electronically or Have Them Mailed to the Bank.** In the case of collecting fees, there need be no person at all. The best practice for assessments and other regular fees or fees from the members is to have a lock box at the bank. The funds are mailed directly to the lock box and processed by the bank. In this way, no board member or manager ever handles the funds. Another way in which a similar arrangement can be achieved is through an on-line payment system. Most professional management companies prefer this arrangement because it limits their chance of mishandling HOA funds. If your management company does not handle your funds in this manner, ask them to set up a lock box at the bank for you.

- **Use Two People to Collect the Money.** For all fees collected on site, the best practice would be to make sure that the person who collects these funds does not have access to the accounting system. Preferably two people would count the money. If they use a calculator with a tape, a tape should be kept as the money is counted. The record should itemize each check and give a total for the deposit. Each person should sign off on the agreed-upon amount collected.

- **The Bookkeeper Records the Funds on the Books.** Once the money has been collected and totaled, it must be recorded in the books of the HOA. As a protection against clerical mistakes or embezzlement, the person who records the funds on the books should not be the same person as the one who collected the money. Once again, the money should be counted before it is recorded, and the bookkeeper should reassure themselves that the amount of cash they received matches that on the tape or the statement from those who collected it.

- **A Third Person Deposits the Money.** While we recognize that this might not always happen, we do recommend that the money be deposited by someone other than the bookkeeper or the treasurer who put the money on the books. Again, this is to assure the board that the person did not alter the amount when her or she recorded it on the books and then deposit a lower amount, pocketing the rest. Once the deposit is made, the deposit slip should be returned to the bookkeeper, showing that the deposit matches the amount collected and the amount recorded.

The board now has a complete paper trail from the time the money was received by the HOA to the point it was deposited. If the board ever has a question about a deposit, a professional management company should be able to provide you with these three pieces of paper, so that any error can be traced and corrected. Again, it is important to make sure that these or similar procedures are followed by your management company when handling your funds.

Once the board has assured itself that the proper procedures are in place, its oversight should be able to stop at the four essential reports we mentioned in the previous chapter. Proactive boards can exercise effective oversight by looking at the trends shown on the income statement and the balance sheet. Sudden disparities in cash compared to last year or unexpected changes in expenses need to be explained clearly by the manager. If she or he cannot provide a cogent reason for the change, the board should dig deeper.

Distributing Funds

For distributing funds from the accounts of an HOA, the same principle applies as did for receiving funds. The custody, recording, and authorization should all be done by separate individuals whenever possible. The same trust created when deposits are handled in this fashion also applies to the money spent.

When an invoice arrives:

1. The manager should sign off on its payment.

2. Then the management company bookkeeper prepares the check and records the withdrawal.

3. The CFO or some other person signs the check.

We recognize this as an ideal situation. If your management company cannot meet this standard for some reason, the board should retain some of the financial authority for itself. For instance, it might be that the treasurer signs the checks. If the unsigned checks are accompanied by an invoice (or better yet the treasurer gets their own copies), then they can verify that the amounts are correct and authorize payment, assured that the HOA's money is going where it should go.

We are big believers in letting a professional manager do their job. While we do want to have procedures in place for the board to oversee their work, it makes sense for the management company to have limited check-writing authority on the HOA's operating account, since it will be responsible for making sure things like the electric bills get paid.

Your governing documents should define how much the management company is allowed to spend before having to seek board approval. Also, the management company should be required to account for the money it spends each month. This is why the income statement to budget comparison is so important for the board to review on a regular basis.

Sticking to the core principle of separating financial functions among several individuals, another best practice is to make sure that the person holding the checks doesn't have direct access to the bank statements. For instance, the manager may hold the checks, but the bookkeeper receives the bank statements, and just to reiterate, the board treasurer should always be able to either print their own statements or have them mailed directly to them. This will help make sure that the bank statements presented to the board are not altered or fabricated.

Your budget should also be used to protect yourself from abuse of a manager's check-writing privilege. Questions need to be raised if you find your manager spending money that deviates from the budget, either in amount or in substance. This is why we believe it important for your Income and Expense statement to provide comparisons between the budgeted amounts and the amounts actually spent. Expenditures not included in the budget should be scrutinized carefully.

The governing documents (and some state laws) also define just how money from the reserve accounts can be accessed. Because the amounts available are much larger and they are only accessed occasionally, the restrictions on how the account is accessed should be tighter. In most instances, the board should not allow a management company to have check-writing authority on the reserve account. These checks should also require two signatures. The board should always require that copies of any checks on this account be kept along with the original invoice for the check. It doesn't hurt for the management company to hold the checks for the reserve account as well.

The process for spending money from the reserve account will be similar to the one that we laid out above for operating expenses. However, some steps will involve board members.

1. The board should authorize the expenditure.

2. The manager should initial the invoice to verify the amount authorized.

3. The management company bookkeeper prepares a check and records the withdrawal.

4. The check should then be signed by the board members.

Making sure these kinds of controls are in place will assure the board that money is spent in the fashion laid out in the operating budget and in the reserve study.

Conclusion

As you can see, good cash controls aren't simply nonsense. They have a purpose. They create a transparent system in which the board can rest assured its money is spent properly.

Cash controls are an essential tool to keep the board from moving from crisis to crisis. They allow a forward-thinking board to get back to planning for the future and getting things done for the HOA.

Thirteen: Reserve Studies

Here is where the rubber meets the road. Throughout this book, we have talked about becoming a board with vision and direction, a proactive board that doesn't spend its time moving from crisis to crisis. How you fund your long-term obligations is the best measure of how you run your HOA. HOAs that fail to plan for major long-term expenses do not handle day-to-day HOA business very well, either. The two go hand in hand. Those HOAs without adequate reserves keep fees unrealistically low. As a result, services are starved, maintenance lags, and curb appeal suffers. Curb appeal directly impacts market value of the homes, so in a real sense, owners are cutting their own throats.

There is a fundamental conflict of interest at work here: The long-term financial and maintenance needs of the community conflict with the individual homeowner's short-term desire to hang on to the money. A homeowner living in a stand-alone home has the luxury or misfortune of doing business this way, while an HOA will fail miserably if it does.

Getting things going in the right direction starts with the board. In a few chapters, we are going to discuss a simple budgeting process that demystifies the process of setting annual assessments. A professional reserve study is a core component of our budgeting process, and that starts with a board adopting a philosophy of saving for tomorrow's big expenses.

The best way to solidify that philosophy is with the adoption of a reserves resolution. This resolution reflects the desire of owners to do long-range reserve planning and funding. Such a resolution curbs the impulses of some boards to "raid the cookie jar" by misspending reserve money or failing to add to reserves when the plan clearly calls for it. A reserves resolution is a critical step toward proper care of the community.

The core of any reserves resolution is a commitment to producing and implementing a thirty-year reserve study. A reserve study is a scientific approach to analyzing future repair and replacement needs and charting a maintenance and funding plan that the board, the manager, and members can follow with ease. It answers the bottom-line question "How much is enough?" and it is an essential component of every budgeting process.

Most importantly, the funding plan should share costs fairly among all owners, not just the poor suckers who get stuck at special assessment time. If your neighbor moves out while your HOA is stuck with backward thinking about reserve funding, he escapes, and it's those left standing who will be left to pay the bill for poor planning and deferred maintenance.

On the other hand, HOAs who take a long-term view do things when they need doing. The place will look so good, you'll never want to move!

A Basic Tutorial

So just what is a reserve study, anyway? Simply put, a reserve study is an estimate of the replacement costs for all components maintained by the HOA for an extended period of time, usually thirty years. The reserve study analyzes repair and replacement needs like roofing and painting that happen on a regular and predictable basis and provides a funding plan for accumulating money to perform this work when it's needed. It is more a budgeting function than a construction or building analysis, although there is an element of that. The study is usually based on visual observations as opposed to forensic testing (tearing components apart to see what's underneath). It assumes that regular and adequate maintenance is being done to prevent premature repairs or replacements.

Creating a reserve study is a two-step process. Funding the reserve study is a third step, which we will cover in its own section of this chapter.

Step One - Make a list of all common and limited common elements that are the HOA's responsibility. These are defined in your HOA's governing documents. Some examples include: decks/patios, gutters & downspouts, roofing, siding repair, elevator renovation, fire protection equipment, pavement overlayment & sealcoating, restriping, pool equipment, furniture, pool replastering, fences, and signage. (Remember that component list we created in our maintenance chapter? It will come in handy here.)

To ensure a thorough list, consider all structures on the property, not just the most obvious ones. For example, unit roofs are obvious, but don't overlook garages, clubhouse, and shed roofs. If similar items are built or placed in service in the same year, lump them together as a single line item and note the total number of items; if not, list them as separate line items. This will be the case in HOAs that were built in phases.

Avoid combining similar components with differing useful lives. Separating these gives a more accurate picture of your reserve funding needs.

Document any assumptions made to eliminate confusion. Proper documentation allows future boards to understand the report. For instance: "Although a common element, the boat dock is not being reserved. It was decided by an HOA vote to remove the dock at the end of its useful life. Refer to the May 2001 annual meeting minutes."

Step Two - Determine the life expectancy and replacement cost. These items go together. Check HOA records for work that has been done to determine an item's life expectancy and replacement cost. If the developer is still available, request construction detail and cost information. If you are in an older development, ask qualified contractors. Some contractors may require a nominal fee for a detailed estimate. However, most will credit payment for an estimate toward any work done within a reasonable time frame. You can also obtain costs for labor, material, and useful lives through cost-estimating resources like RS Means or Craftsman Books, which provide national averages indexed to your local area. This is typically sufficient for long-range planning. If you use national averages, always get a detailed estimate near the end of the useful life of a component for a more accurate picture.

Once you have a projection of your expenses for the next thirty years, it's time to fund your plan.

Funding Your Reserve Study

Unfortunately, many more associations have a reserve study than actually fund a reserve study. That's like buying a car but refusing to purchase gas: It'll go nowhere. The reserve study should provide a recommended funding plan that calls for regular and adequate contributions to pay for future repairs without the need for special assessments. For common wall communities, this is usually accomplished monthly. For HOAs with few assets, reserve contributions can be made quarterly or annually, whatever the regular fee schedule is. If each member contributes a portion monthly, all members that own in the community during the thirty-year time line will only contribute an amount equal to their time of ownership. And all members should pay their share of reserves. As we said in the introduction, this is by far the fairest way to approach to reserve funding.

We will go into further detail on how to use your reserve study in your annual budgeting process in a different chapter. For now we want to answer a few basic questions.

- **How should these reserve funds be accounted for?** Reserve funds should be kept separate from operating funds. If your reserve plan is complete (includes all components and a plan to fund them), establishing separate ledger accounts for each component is unnecessary. The board should only spend out of reserves for items that are included in the component list.

- **How should the reserve funds be invested?** It's conceivable that reserves could grow to many thousands, or even millions, of dollars. Since the reserve study shows the board when reserve funds will be needed, unused funds can be placed in higher-yielding long-term investments. Every dollar earned in interest is one less dollar needed from the members. Increasing interest yield only 1% over thirty years can amount to tens of thousands of dollars for the average HOA. If an HOA is large and accumulating hundreds of thousands or millions of dollars in reserves, it makes sense to hire a professional investment advisor to manage the funds. Conservative investments like government securities or certificates of deposit (CDs) are recommended. However, there are other options that an advisor can recommend.

- **Percent Funded.** A quality reserve study will compare what reserve funds you currently have to what you should have. Along the thirty-year reserve study timeline, there is an ideal amount of money the HOA should set aside, called 100% or "full funding." The percentage of funding listed in the reserve study shows how the HOA is doing relative to the ideal. For example, it is not uncommon for an older HOA that has not properly funded its reserves to be 20% funded or less. Knowing the current percentage of your reserve needs that you have set aside is essential to chart a plan to catch up. You need to know where you are to know where you need to go. If your HOA is newer, the sooner you perform a reserve study and begin funding it, the sooner you will reach the 100% funded ideal.

• **How often should the reserve study be updated?** Once the initial reserve study is completed and the funding plan is in place, yearly updates need to be performed. These are relatively simple to do. Even if no reserve projects are done, the rate of inflation and the yield on invested funds always change year to year. Even a 1% change in either of these factors causes a huge impact on the thirty-year projection, due to interest compounding.

• **What happens if reserves are under-funded?** It depends. If the HOA has inadequate reserve funds to begin with, the reserve study will show the need for "catch up." How fast the HOA catches up depends on how soon funds are needed. If there is an expensive and urgent repair like roofing, a special assessment will be needed to address it. If major repairs are some years off, the funding plan can usually accrue the money through regular assessments (fees). Using a combination of both special and regular assessments may instead be the way to go. Whatever course of action is taken, the goal should be to reach "100% funding."

Who to Hire and How Much It Costs

Very rarely will an HOA have the expertise among its members to do a proper thirty-year reserve study. Too often, plans created in-house miss important components, leaving the HOA chronically under-funded and vulnerable to the dreaded special assessment. Reserve studies are best left to a professional. Hire a professional from the Association of Professional Reserve Analysts. Its members hold the highest credential in the reserve study industry, Professional Reserve Analyst (PRA). Even if the HOA board believes it has the expertise to do its own study, there are clear advantages to having a reserve study professional perform the work. Aside from the expertise, knowledge of local contractors, and current costs, a professional does not have the conflict of interest that HOA members have. (Remember that section in the insurance chapter on limiting your liability?)

Besides considerable experience doing reserve studies and a list of satisfied HOA client references, a qualified reserve study provider should have credentials, good budgeting skills, and extensive knowledge of construction and HOA operations.

So how much does a reserve study cost? Costs to perform a reserve study vary according to the size of the HOA, the number of components, and the time needed for fieldwork and report compilation. The initial reserve study costs the most, since it involves fieldwork and time to gather the component data. Reserve study costs typically range from $1500 to $4000 for HOAs up to 100 units (although extraordinary circumstances, number of components, or high-cost locations can drive cost higher). Large communities with many reserve components can expect to pay tens of thousands of dollars. If there are particular problems like dry rot, structural damage, or soil or drainage issues, an engineering study should be incorporated with the reserve study. Recommended annual updates are much less costly, since they involve only tweaking the initial study assumptions.

Reviewed Annually

While thirty-year plans are dandy, thirty years is a long time, and things can happen that are impossible to predict. Inflation moves up and down, as does return on invested reserves. Construction costs can be higher or lower based on competition, the state of the real estate market, and the price of oil from the Middle East (talk about unpredictable!).

One of the biggest wild cards in this thirty-year projection is how well preventive maintenance is done. Preventive maintenance addresses those little things that, if left undone, have huge impact on a component's useful life. For example, if a roof is not kept clean of moss, or does not have small seam separations repaired, the normal useful life could easily be cut in half. Siding that is not inspected, repaired, and caulked on a regular basis can fail years sooner than it should. Failure to perform regular and adequate preventive maintenance can undermine the reserve study's prognostications.

How well the board invests reserve funds also has enormous impact on the funding model. Improving the rate of return an average of only one to two percent over the thirty-year period can reduce owner contributions by thousands of dollars (in HOAs with extensive assets, hundreds of thousands of dollars).

The message is clear: A reserve plan is an essential planning tool for all HOAs but, to be truly useful, must be refined over time. It's like tending a vineyard. Left untended, the fruit (value) will gradually disappear.

The annual budget review is the logical time to assess the condition of the reserve plan. A judgment should be made on the life and cost assumptions of each component included in the plan. Do they still hold true, or is there need for some revision? This is the time to go back to the professional who did your original plan and seek help in making sure the plan is up to date.

Are there new components that need to be added, like a major landscape or sprinkler system renovation? As the saying goes, "Change is inevitable (except from vending machines)," and this is particularly true about reserve plans.

Conclusion

The fiduciary responsibility of the board is to preserve the home values of the members. This task is for all practical purposes impossible without a reserve study to help the board estimate just what future expenses it will face. On the one hand, a conscientious board without such a plan might find it is over-funding its reserves based on fear instead of fact. Far more likely, it will find that in the name of keeping costs "reasonable" for its members, it has under-funded its reserves. Such boards need to ask how "reasonable" the next special assessment will feel. Today is the day to get this right. Just like a family's emergency fund, HOA reserves keep the next predictable "emergency" from becoming a disaster.

Fourteen: Handling Special Assessments

There isn't a particularly tactful way to say this. Well-run HOAs almost never use special assessments to cover either predictable maintenance or unexpected repairs. Don't despair. Most often, the boards that must implement a special assessment are only cleaning up years of mess over which they had no control.

So how do you implement a special assessment should one become necessary, and how do you ensure that one never becomes necessary again in the future? These are the questions this chapter will tackle.

When Should We Do a Special Assessment?

Special assessments should always be a last resort, used only in the direst of circumstances. First, as we said in the chapter on reserve studies, a special assessment is an unfair way of paying for needed maintenance. It's also the most expensive. By using reserves, the HOA forgoes up to thirty years of interest payments on its money, which even in safe investments is no small amount. If mishandled, special assessments are incredibly divisive. There is no better way for a board to bring out the tar and feathers in an HOA than to suggest a special assessment.

For all these reasons, we believe there are really only two circumstances in which an HOA might consider a special assessment. First, and most obviously, a special assessment might become necessary when urgent repair issues are causing accelerated damage and must be taken care of immediately.

Second, in a few instances, an HOA might find it necessary to use a special assessment if it has a large amount of delinquent payments from members. In general, delinquent fees should not be used as an excuse for a special assessment. Instead they should motivate the board to begin an aggressive collections program. Unfortunately, such programs can take a long time, and especially if there is some kind of fiscal emergency, a special assessment might become necessary. Also, a special assessment lien on a unit might be the only way to collect money from the unit if it is in foreclosure.

While there may be a few exceptions here or there, in almost all other circumstances, boards should attempt to solve their financial dilemmas without resorting to a special assessment.

Talking to Your Membership

Remember the earlier chapter on communicating with your members? Nothing will test how well you have learned the lessons of that chapter like a special assessment. The crowds who attend a meeting to discuss a special assessment can carry torches and pitchforks. Many want someone to blame. Make sure to hold a members forum before the official board meeting, where each member can speak their mind. Let them express their fears and frustrations. If the assessment is large enough, some of them might even lose their homes.

Once the members have expressed their concerns, it is important that the board clearly lay out the necessity for the special assessment. Here are four key points that should be expressed clearly to the members.

1. **Immediate Repairs Are Necessary.** When deferred maintenance threatens the common property of the HOA, clearly explain that the assessment is necessary to prevent a larger bill later if the damage is allowed to continue.

2. **Members' Home Values Are Threatened.** Remind members that the value of their homes is directly tied to the value of the common property.

3. **Maintenance Is Necessary to Sell Homes.** Remind members that proper maintenance and adequate reserves help buyers qualify for loans. Many lenders require the HOA to have reserves to approve buyer loans. Homes in HOAs that have

reserves are worth more than those that don't and will sell for higher prices.

4. **The Board Is Fixing Old Problems.** While diplomacy and tact are called for in such circumstances, it is important that the board explain to the membership that it is picking up the pieces for years of mismanagement (if true). These problems didn't arise on your watch. You are only trying to fix them.

Often a special assessment becomes a clarion call for a community to get its financial house in order. If you find yourself looking down the barrel of one, don't miss the opportunity to make clear to the residents that things are going to have to change to make sure this is a one-time event and not the beginning of a pattern for your community.

Paying for a Special Assessment

When it comes to paying for a special assessment, we recommend that the board avoid taking out a loan. First of all, this is the most expensive way to fund a special assessment. These loans carry high interest rates and closing costs—much higher rates than the loans available to individual members. It also puts the HOA in the role of the lender, having to collect payments from members who might default on those payments. This isn't exactly great for the harmony of your HOA, which is already naturally strained by the assessment itself.

A better practice is for HOAs to pay for the needed repairs and then assess the members the full amount. Most members have access to much cheaper sources of capital, including savings, home equity loans, credit cards, and Uncle Harry. This will allow your members to pursue the means they have available and keep the HOA from having to deal with collecting payments.

Preventing Special Assessments

As the saying goes, an ounce of prevention is worth a pound of cure. The path away from special assessments and toward a forward-thinking board becomes obvious when you recognize that special assessments result from only one cause—a lack of reserve funding. The leaky roof may come suddenly, but the fact that the roof was going to need repairs was known to the board for the last three decades. So the board that wants to prevent special assessments needs to do only one thing—reserve a proper amount for repairs on a regular basis.

As we discussed in the previous chapter, a proper reserve study will tell the board how much it needs to save each year for future repairs. However, the reserve study is only useful if it is used as part of a board's annual budgeting process. In the next chapter, we will go into more detail on how to incorporate your reserve study into your planning for next year's budget. Finally, a properly produced and funded reserve study isn't worth the paper it is written on if the HOA has a large number of delinquent owners. A board needs to work with the manager to deal aggressively with delinquent owners in order to make sure it doesn't find itself asking those who do pay to pay more while those who haven't paid slip further behind.

Catching Up Without Using a Special Assessment

Special assessments can be incredibly damaging to community morale, not to mention personal finances. Almost by definition, they result when not enough reserves have been set aside in the past to cover the needs of the present. This isn't a surprise. Usually the board knows that it is shorting reserves for years before the assessment becomes necessary.

So what do you do if you are on a board that realizes it has to change its ways? Should it ask for the special assessment now to catch up on its reserve plan?

In most cases, we think it is better for the board to set up a funding plan that ramps up to 100% funding over several years, rather than to use a special assessment to catch up all at once. Special assessments are sometimes difficult or impossible to collect. They should be saved for urgent repairs that occur before the board catches up.

Instead, we recommend a funding model that takes an HOA's current level of funding into account.

- **5-30% Funded.** Ramp up to 100% funding in twenty to thirty years

- **30%-60% Funded**. Ramp up in fifteen to twenty years

- **Over 60% Funded**. Ramp up in five to ten years

A funding plan like this recognizes that the problem built up over a series of years. It also puts the current owners on notice that fees are going up every year until reserves reach 100% funding. We have never had a problem selling this approach to the boards we advise.

For proactive boards that want to avoid larger problems down the road, the moral of the story is to start turning the ship around today. It only gets more costly and more difficult the longer you wait. It's time that you fully fund your reserve study each and every year. That will be the topic of our next chapter, on budgeting.

Fifteen:
Making Budgets Easy

How do you know how well you did last year as a board, and, more importantly, how do you clearly articulate that to your members? We consistently find boards struggling with both of these questions when it comes time to do the annual budget. Most board members want to do the right thing and fully fund reserves. However, they find it difficult to communicate to members why the HOA appears to be assessing far more than it spent on operating expenses each year. This lack of clear communication hampers a board's ability to assess the fees necessary to fully fund reserves.

The tendency is to compromise. Rather than basing their budgets on their needed reserves, boards will often base their assessments on what they believe their membership can afford. A regular habit of under-funding budgets always leads to problems down the road, including special assessments and sudden increases in fees. While we recognize that these may happen from time to time, they should be avoided whenever possible. In this chapter, we want to give you the tools you need to confidently set your annual assessments where they should be and to communicate to your membership the reasons for your decision.

A forward-thinking budget starts with asking the question: What are the expenses we need to cover in the next year? Once boards focus their budgeting around answering this question, the pieces fall into place.

This is, of course, different than the question for-profit businesses or families need to ask when they sit down to budget. They need to start their healthy financial thinking in a different place because what they spend is dictated by what they bring in.

On the other hand, HOA boards have a mandate to manage the business of the HOA. Many of the expenses are fixed. Landscaping, building maintenance, and the pool must be paid for each year (unless the members approve closing the pool). This responsibility also includes reserving for maintenance and replacement of components in the future. Fees should be set to meet the real costs of running the HOA, not on the finances of the individual members.

This transition away from asking "what can the members afford?" to "what are the real expenses?" can be difficult for boards who have not done this in the past. At some point, all boards who have been charging what their members "could afford," rather than what they needed to charge, will have to switch their thinking. Hopefully, they do so before the special assessment becomes necessary.

Fund Accounting

The fees collected by an HOA have two purposes. The homeowners pay fees to: a.) make sure that the HOA is providing common areas and amenities that operate properly in the present, and b.) make sure that these common areas and amenities are adequately maintained in the future.

A board that wants to avoid special assessments and understand its financial health needs to keep these two pools of money separate from each other. It won't do to purchase new picnic tables and do little remodeling projects on an annual basis if it means that a special assessment will be necessary down the road for painting the buildings.

Keeping these pools of money separate is also the foundation of a healthy budgeting process, and the financial statements you receive from your manager should reflect this separation as well. In the accounting industry, this practice is called "fund accounting."

On a basic level, most boards understand the need for some kind of fund accounting. They have both an operating account and a reserve account, intended for long-term maintenance projects. We would argue that this separation should carry through to the budgeting process. In essence, the HOA doesn't have one budget. It has two, and the process for creating each is slightly different. The HOA has an operating budget, which covers all the expenses the HOA will face over the coming year. It also has a reserve budget, which collects money in the current year for maintenance expenses down the road. When such major remodeling or repairs become necessary in the current year, this budget shows how you will spend your reserves. The final master budget is simply a combination of these two smaller budgets.

Creating separate budgets for operating expenses and reserves also helps make sure boards know that they haven't either overcharged or undercharged the members. Boards who create only a master budget that combines both their operating expenses and their reserve savings can tend to want to lower fees because they mistakenly believe they have brought in a large surplus at the end of a given year. The opposite can be true when they spend money on reserve items. They may believe their annual deficit means they need to raise their fees when it does not. Keeping two separate budgets helps avoid these problems.

For some HOAs, fund accounting may go well beyond simply keeping track of what money comes in for operating expenses and what money comes in for reserves. For example, perhaps an HOA has a golf course that costs a large amount to maintain each year but also generates some revenue. Such an HOA would do well to keep the expenses and income for the golf course separate from the expenses and income from other areas of operations on the financial reports. Come budgeting time, fund accounting will allow this HOA to quickly determine if the revenue generated by the golf course is enough to offset a portion or all of the expenses it costs the HOA. Perhaps it needs to raise the public green fees or find ways to reduce its expenses. It would be very difficult for this HOA to have any understanding of its need if the expenses for the golf course were mashed together with the rest of the operating budget. Every board that wants to have a clear picture of the health of its organization should make sure that services that generate significant revenue—such as public swimming pools or golf courses—are shown separately on the financial reports throughout the year. During the creation of the budget, each of these sources of income should be examined separately to determine their effect on the overall health of the HOA.

How to Create Operating and Reserve Budgets

An HOA operating budget covers all the items on which the board will spend money in the next year. The goal for this budget is to take in from the members the exact amount in fees that the board expects to spend over the next twelve months, plus a small amount for contingencies such as unexpected cost increases.

In most cases, the operating budget is not at all difficult to calculate, because the items on which a board spends money are fairly consistent from year to year. There should be some slight adjustment to this budget for cost increases each year, and there may be changes because the board has changed the way in which it manages the HOA. However, most items in the operating budget can usually carry forward from last year.

Running your HOA on an accrual basis pays dividends when budgeting, since it takes into account events that have not yet occurred. However, many boards and managers using an accrual basis for their financial reports fall back to cash-based thinking when they budget. This can cause a couple of problems. First, they often can seriously overestimate their income in the coming year. An accrual-based financial statement may rightly show that only half of the receivables will be collected in the next year. However, boards that used a cash-based budgeting process may forget this when they budget. On the other hand, the opposite can also be the case. A board that does not take receivables into account may overcharge on assessments, leading to some very unhappy members and trouble down the road.

One other little hiccup in the budgeting process is created by the depreciation of HOA assets. If you remember from our previous chapter, an HOA owns the personal property of the HOA—items like the television, the refrigerator, and the couches in the common room. These items show up as assets of the HOA on the operating budget. Each year these items will go down in value. When it comes to budgeting time, this loss in value will be recorded as depreciation on the operating budget. However, boards need to remember that saving for a new television, refrigerator, and couch will all be part of their reserve budget because these items are not replaced annually. As a result, some HOAs' operating budgets appear to run at a loss on a year-to-year basis. This is OK, as long as the loss is created by the depreciation of personal property.

The reserve budget should be even less complicated for the board, as the amount charged to members for reserves is the amount their reserve study tells them to save over the next year. As we said in the last chapter, proper budgeting for reserves is a major reason to get a professional reserve study done.

The reserve budget will always cover major repairs and replacements. However, the extent to which a reserve study will account for smaller repairs will vary by the study. Boards should make sure they include some kind of contingency for repairs in the budget if their reserve study does not add it in for them.

The final master budget is created by simply combining the operating budget for the next year with the reserve budget and any other budgets created by the board. A board that creates its master budget in this way can rest assured that it has taken good care of its HOA's finances.

Budget Oversight

While many boards get themselves deep into the budgeting process, some allow their manager to prepare a proposed budget for them that they approve and then present to their members. We believe that letting the expert manager prepare a budget allows the board to spend its time elsewhere, and this is a good thing.

However, a board that allows its manager to create its budget needs to be willing to exercise oversight. Here are three steps that will help you meet your responsibilities to your HOA.

- **Ask Your Manager to Present Separate Budgets.** Separate reserve and operating budgets make it much easier to understand the financial health of your HOA, and it will make it much easier to propose to your members. You may be required by your governing documents or by law to present to your members a master budget that shows all the expenses in one budget, but there is no reason you cannot also present them with budgets that show the expenses broken down into their components.

- **The Reserve Budget Should Match Your Reserve Study.** This is vital to avoid special assessments down the road. It is always a good idea to save a little extra to handle anything unexpected that may come up.

- **Compare the Operating Budget With Last Year's Budget** Make sure that a.) expenses didn't simply roll forward without adjustment, and b.) there are good explanations for any significant changes to the list of expenses included in this year's budget.

Communicating With Your Members

For boards that would desire to fully fund their reserves without a rebellion, great communication is key. We went over many ideas for clear communication in an earlier chapter, but boards so often seem to have trouble justifying their assessments to members that we felt it important to make a couple of concrete suggestions here.

Even if they don't get confused themselves, boards that do only a single master budget have a much more difficult time communicating to their members why an organization that isn't designed to make a profit takes in so much more than it spends on an annual basis. Keeping the reserve budget separate from the operating budget helps clarify the assessment you have given them.

While most boards are required by the state or by their own governing documents to create and present a budget to their members, there is nothing to stop a board from then breaking that budget apart and also presenting both an operating budget and a separate reserve budget. This will clearly demonstrate the reasons why the board assesses the fees it does, and that those fees are necessary to fund reserves and meet the upcoming year's anticipated expenses.

Communication about the budget can't start at the annual meeting when the board is presenting the budget to the members. It has to start well before then. Newsletters are a great place to take the time to explain the budgeting process and the reserve study. They can also be places where a board can explain the consequences created by special assessments and the steps the board is taking to avoid them.

More importantly, invoices can also be an important means for communicating with members. Boards should ask their management company to prepare invoices that separate assessments collected for operating expenses and assessments collected for reserves. This way, members are reminded throughout the year that not all the money collected will be spent in this year. Instead, some will be placed in reserve for the future. This will go a long way to prepare members to understand the budget when it is presented later in the year.

An executive summary of the budget should always be presented with the budget to the members. This summary should explain the budgeting process to the members and explain that while the operating budget is designed to be as lean as possible, the reserve budget is designed to save for future expenses, so in most years it will not spend all that it takes in. It should also explain that the amount designated for reserves was recommended by a professional, independent reserve study and not the whims of the board. (You did get a reserve study, didn't you?) It should clearly show the amount proposed for next year's assessment and explain how much is designated for reserves and how much for operating expenses. If your HOA finds itself under-funded on its reserves, the summary should also explain how the HOA plans to make up the deficit.

All of this communication tells your members that you respect their money and will take as little of it as possible to meet the obligations of the HOA. Remind them that board members pay their fair share as well. It also lays the groundwork for your team of experts to answer questions at the annual meeting, whether that team is simply your manager or includes a CPA, as well.

Conclusion

Budgeting is often intimidating to boards that don't have a clear understanding of how to approach it. Too many boards make the mistake of thinking too much like a business in this area, asking "how much can we charge?" rather than "what expenses need to be covered?" Once they ask the right question and separate out the reserve budget from the operating budget, the process makes sense. It also makes the communication with your members clear and much more convincing, and this makes the job of being a board member much more enjoyable.

Sixteen:
Yes, Virginia, HOAs Do Pay Taxes

Although it may sound surprising to many HOA boards, we do run into some boards that have unexpectedly found themselves in trouble because they haven't filed a federal tax return. Recently, we received a panicked call from an HOA whose reserves had been levied by the IRS for back taxes and penalties because it hadn't filed a tax return last year. Let's make this clear up front: Every HOA must file a tax return on an annual basis, even if it doesn't owe any tax.

Sometimes in the midst of a board transition, the tax return can get missed. In other cases, the boards believe they don't have to file because they are a "non-profit" organization (which they usually aren't, but that's another matter). In previous chapters, we talked about creating an annual calendar for maintenance and HOA events, such as the annual meeting. We suggest that filing the tax return should also go on that calendar.

Part of the confusion arises because, in general, the IRS does not tax the assessments of an HOA when those assessments are used for the core purposes of the association—in this case, the management of the HOA and the maintenance of the common property. This is not the same as the IRS saying that an HOA is a non-profit in the tax code. HOAs do not typically file the same paperwork or tax forms as a non-profit, like a church or charitable organization. The IRS still views HOAs like corporations. However, the IRS declares most HOAs to be corporations without a profit motive.

The IRS has recognized the value and legitimacy of HOAs by creating a separate type of corporate tax form with its own rules just for HOAs that do not have a profit motive. The vast majority of HOAs file form 1120H. This form exempts all member assessments from taxation. However, this does not mean that these HOAs will not pay any taxes. These organizations will still pay taxes on incidental income, such as the fees from the laundry facility, the interest earned on their bank accounts, or fees charged to members for using the community room, even if the HOA files form 1120H.

It isn't uncommon for a board, at the end of the year, to have extra money left over which came from one of these other income sources—for example, money from its community room rentals. Many boards that file form 1120H want to do the right thing with this extra money, so they will save that money for a rainy day by putting it in their reserves. This is a great decision, as long as they remember that this income is still taxable. Problems can arise when these HOAs or their accountants treat all income the same, simply because they file form 1120H.

This is another reason why HOAs should use fund accounting practices on their financial reports. Fund accounting should be used to keep unrelated business income separated from member's fees, which are not taxed for these HOAs. This can help the board get a rough estimate on the amount of tax it will pay at the end of the year.

The IRS does have its limits. Sometimes the unrelated business income of an HOA will become so large that the IRS argues that the HOA is really more of a business rather than an association. When this happens, the IRS treats the HOA exactly like a for-profit corporation and forces it to file tax form 1120. For these HOAs, member fees are not automatically exempted from taxation. They are presumed taxable unless proved otherwise.

Most often, HOAs that have to file form 1120 are quite large and complex, with things like golf courses or other high-revenue activities that aren't directly related to the core purposes of the association. However, this doesn't always have to be the case. Sometimes small HOAs get a large percentage of their income from the interest on their reserves. This is particularly true of older condominiums that have saved wisely, but haven't done any major renovations. Occasionally, this investment income can be enough to disqualify the HOA from filing form 1120H. The other common reason HOAs must file form 1120 is that they do not file their taxes on time, and the IRS will no longer allow them to file form 1120H.

The proper financial management of HOAs that must file form 1120 is well beyond the scope of this book. Such an HOA will need to put a team of experts in place to make sure it organizes its finances appropriately. For instance, while most HOAs can be content with only two bank accounts, one for operating expenses and one for reserves, an HOA that files form 1120 will need to have three bank accounts, one for its operating expenses, one for its capital reserves, and another for its non-capital reserves. Fund accounting is essential for an 1120 HOA, although how these HOAs set up their various funds will be quite different than the process we described in this book. We could go on, but we won't. Suffice it to say, if you believe that you will end up filing form 1120, it is essential that you work only with managers who have specific experience and expertise in handling large HOAs like yours. You will also need to work closely with a CPA who has specific experience handling 1120 HOAs.

There are three tests to see whether you qualify for form 1120H or for form 1120. These tests will be the topic of our next section.

The Three Tests

The IRS recognizes that HOAs don't exist in order to make a profit. This is why it has created form 1120H specifically for HOAs. However, the IRS also realizes the temptations of the loopholes it creates. It has a vested interest in making sure that a for-profit real estate development corporation doesn't disguise itself as an HOA and thus avoid paying taxes on its profits. It has devised three tests that help sort out those HOAs that truly function without a direct profit motive and those that act like for-profit companies and must pay taxes like any other corporation. The following are the three tests used by the IRS to determine if an HOA will qualify to file form 1120H.

1. The organization must be a condominium management association, a residential real estate association, or a time-share association.

2. Sixty percent of the association's gross income must consist of exempt function income. Exempt function income consists of membership dues, assessments, and fees paid as homeowners of the association. The fees a member pays are exempt from taxes only if they are paid by virtue of being a member of the organization. Fees are taxable if the member is acting as a

customer of the HOA. For instance, the fees a member pays to rent the common room for a family function or any fees paid by members to use laundry facilities are taxable and should be handled accordingly. The IRS states it this way: "[Exempt function income] must come from members as owners not as customers of the association." ("2013 Instructions for Form 1120-H." IRS.gov. January 1, 2013. Accessed October 21, 2014.) All other income is taxable income in this test and on form 1120H.

Proactive HOAs can do a little tax planning here. Let's say your HOA has a small, private golf course open only to homeowners. Perhaps the green fees are troublesome because they cause the HOA to fail this test and force it to file form 1120, creating a much more complicated HOA with much higher accounting and tax expenses. If the board changed the HOA's structure and charged every member of the HOA a maintenance fee for the golf course and then allowed them a certain number of free rounds per month, it could save the HOA thousands in taxes by allowing it to pass this test and file form 1120H.

Even HOAs that already qualify for form 1120H may be able to save some in taxes by getting rid of extra fees charged to members for use of the common room or the tennis courts and instead paying for maintenance of such common areas with the member's assessments. Remember, member's assessments are exempt from taxation and help the HOA avoid filing form 1120. Fees paid by members are taxable.

3. At least ninety percent of the association's expenses must be spent to acquire, build, manage, maintain, and care for the property of the association.

This test can appear quite easy to meet but can get complicated quickly. It is the test that most frequently eliminates an HOA from qualifying for form 1120H. For instance, a board that has a small, public pool may ask its on-site manager to act as the pool manager, hiring the lifeguards etc. When tax time comes, the pool may show a large, taxable profit. In order to avoid taxes on that money, it may choose to allocate some percentage of the manager's salary as an expense to offset the profits on the pool. However, that piece of the manager's salary may no longer qualify for the ninety percent rule. This HOA may find itself filing form 1120 instead of 1120H.

Filing form 1120 isn't always a bad financial decision for an HOA. It may be better to offset the pool profits with the manager's salary, even though it means filing form 1120. It may actually save the HOA money. However, in most instances, it will be far preferable for the HOA to file form 1120H, saving hundreds if not thousands of dollars in unwanted taxes.

Confused yet? We recognize that very few people who sign up to volunteer for the board of an HOA do so because they want to spend hours of their time figuring out just which tax form to file and how they could set up their organization in the most effective manner possible. This is again another place where an HOA would be wise to find an outside expert—in this case, a CPA with HOA experience—who can help them organize their HOA so as to avoid paying unneeded taxes to the government.

Taxes are yet another good reason to make sure your financial house is kept in good order. Poor financial statements and late tax filings will inevitably cost your board money down the road. Proactive boards endeavor to avoid this at all costs.

Seventeen: Conclusion

So where are you as an HOA board? How do you stack up against the ideals in this book? Are you a well-oiled machine dedicated to serving your members or are you caught in a reactive cycle, bouncing from crisis to crisis? Most boards fall somewhere in between. They muddle along, getting some things right but missing badly in other areas.

Remember, ineffective practices and denial didn't develop in an instant. Most often an HOA falls into disorder and neglect over a period of years. It takes time to put things right. Little, if anything, can be fixed overnight.

Where you stand is much less important than where you are heading. In this book, we have set out to give you the destination. Now it's up to you to move toward the goal. You won't be able to get there on your own. It will take assistance and buy-in from your members, and at times, you will need outside experts to show you the path.

Is it worth the work? Most definitely. Once you have your systems in place, a well-run HOA is so much easier to manage than one that is crisis driven. Just keep in mind that your job as the board is to lead the organization, not to do the work yourselves. Hire that out to other people or, if appropriate, find members to volunteer.

If you need help, don't hesitate to reach out. We're here, too. We love to hear from board members like you.

With a little diligence and patience, step by step, you can move your HOA further down the path toward the care-free lifestyle promised when you moved in.

Erik Wecks

Erik Wecks is a full time writer and blogger living in Vancouver, Washington. He is the author of the best-selling personal finance book, *How to Manage Your Money When You Don't Have Any*, and the creator of the speculative fiction universe The Pax Imperium. He is a contributor to the GeekDad blog formerly on Wired.com and has contributed to LitReactor.com. He writes on a wide range of topics. When not waxing poetic on various aspects of fiscal responsibility, he tends toward the geeky.

Erik loves to spend time with his family. He is married to an angel, Jaylene, who has taught him more than anyone else about true mercy and compassion. They are the parents of three wonderful girls. As a group they like swimming at the local pool, gardening, reading aloud, playing piano, and beating each other soundly at whatever tabletop game is handy.

You can sign up for Erik's newsletter on his website.

Follow Erik:
Website: www.erikwecks.com
Facebook: www.facebook.com/erikwecks
Twitter: **www.twitter.com/erikwecks**

HOW TO MANAGE YOUR MONEY WHEN YOU DON'T HAVE ANY

ERIK WECKS

Doug McLain

Doug McLain is a CPA living in Vancouver, Washington, and has been auditing homeowner associations since 2001. He is a shareholder with Currie & McLain, P.S., an accounting firm specializing in homeowner association accounting and taxes. He is also a founding partner of HOA Tax Help, the first online tax preparation tool specifically designed for homeowner associations. You can find Doug's thoughts on various homeowner association accounting and tax issues at the Hoataxhelp.com/blog.

Doug's experience with homeowner associations has led him to various volunteer opportunities in the community. He is currently volunteering with the Washington State University business department as a mentor to graduating business students. He has also served as board treasurer for the non-profit Affordable Community Environments (ACE) for several years. In his free time, which is not much during tax season, he enjoys hiking, canoeing, scuba diving, and camping with his family and their border collie.

Doug McLain can be contacted at doug@hoataxhelp.com

1120-H Tax Return Only $99

Prepare your HOA taxes online in 3 easy steps...

1. Gather your information
2. Answer some simple questions
3. Find out if you qualify – Instantly

"Hoataxhelp was developed by CPAs as a low cost alternative for preparing HOA taxes"

Richard Thompson

   Richard has over thirty years experience in real estate sales, construction and property management. Since 1992, his focus has been homeowner association (HOA) management. In 1996, he founded Regenesis to offer financial, maintenance, management, and administrative services to HOA boards, managers, and developers. Some accomplishments:

President:
Regenesis, Inc., an HOA management consulting company

Editor & Publisher:
The Regenesis Report, a monthly HOA newsletter since 1997

Website:
Regenesis.net, world's largest HOA resource (paid subscription)

Online:
RealtyTimes.com (weekly column)

Magazines:
Articles have been published in **Habitat, Money, Community Manager, New England Condominium, Bloomberg Personal Finance, Condo Management, Common Ground** and **Florida Community Association Journal**

Book:
Wrote chapter in Donald Trump's book **"The Best Real Estate Advice I Ever Received"**

Newspapers:
Quoted as HOA Expert in **Wall Street Journal, The Washington Times, Chicago Tribune, Daily Journal of Commerce, Calgary Herald** and many others

Continuing Education Curriculum:
Provides content to **Bert Rodgers School** for Florida community association manager continuing education

Founder:
Oregon Washington Community Association Managers www.OWCAM.org

President:
Association of Professional Reserve Analysts www.apra-usa.com

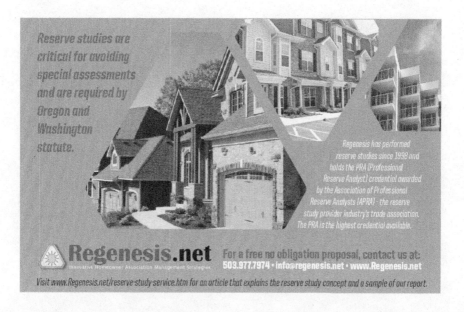

Made in the USA
Monee, IL
03 August 2024